The Story of
CLARA
BARTON
of the RED CROSS

The inspiring story of Clara Barton who, almost single-handed and against terrific odds, formulated the American Red Cross. Against the background of her times, we see her as the little girl growing up in New England, the successful schoolteacher and Patent Office clerk, the "Angel of Mercy" on Civil War battlefields, the valiant heroine of the Franco-Prussian War—and finally, the founder of the American Red Cross, which was the most glorious of her innumerable achievements. It can truly be said about Clara Barton that no other American woman has more nobly embodied those principles and ideals which are the heritage of true patriotism.

Books by

Jeannette Covert Nolan

ABRAHAM LINCOLN

ANDREW JACKSON

BENEDICT ARNOLD
  Traitor to His Country

DOLLEY MADISON

FLORENCE NIGHTINGALE

THE GAY POET
  The Story of Eugene Field

GEORGE ROGERS CLARK
  Soldier and Hero

JOHN BROWN

LA SALLE AND THE GRAND
  ENTERPRISE

THE LITTLE GIANT
  Stephen A. Douglas

O. HENRY
  The Story of William Sydney Porter

THE SHOT HEARD ROUND THE WORLD
  The Story of Lexington and Concord

SPY FOR THE CONFEDERACY
  Rose O'Neal Greenhow

THE STORY OF CLARA BARTON
  OF THE RED CROSS

TREASON AT THE POINT

The Story of

CLARA BARTON

of the RED CROSS

JEANNETTE COVERT NOLAN

JULIAN MESSNER
NEW YORK

PUBLISHED SIMULTANEOUSLY IN THE UNITED STATES AND CANADA BY JULIAN MESSNER, A DIVISION OF SIMON & SCHUSTER, INC., 1 WEST 39 STREET, NEW YORK, N. Y. 10018. ALL RIGHTS RESERVED.

B
Barton

COPYRIGHT, ©, 1941 BY
JEANNETTE COVERT NOLAN
Twentieth Printing, 1967

PRINTED IN THE UNITED STATES OF AMERICA

Part One

Part One

1

M R. STEPHEN BARTON stepped softly from the curtained bedchamber and paused at the window in the hall. The scene framed there was of a winter-locked Massachusetts landscape, hills molded in jackets of snow, cushiony drifts bordering the hard-packed road which led to the village of North Oxford, trees bent under a brittle burden of ice glinting like mica in the brilliant sunlight. A prospect of serenity—and around him the house was quiet, except for a stir, a murmuring in the kitchen. Squaring his shoulders, Mr. Barton strode in that direction.

"Children," he said, from the threshold.

Instantly they turned toward him, Dorothy and Sally stopping in the midst of their task; the boys, Stephen and David, rising from the long bench before the hearth. They did not speak. They waited, caught by the strange quality of their father's manner, an exultant, ringing note in his deep voice.

A big man, erect and handsome in his broadcloth coat, the high starched collar and black satin stock which he donned only for special occasions, he approached the table. He scrutinized the knives and forks, the clean linen cover. He picked up a plate, stared at it. Still the children waited, silently.

"These ordinary things will not suffice." He put down the plate with a decisive clatter. "Take them away, girls. And bring the sterling silver flatware."

3

"But, Father," Sally protested, "Dorothy and I have just finished making the table nice for Christmas!"

"Nice? Yes." He smiled. "Today, though, our table must be *splendid*. We never have had, or are likely to have in future, such a December twenty-fifth as this one in 1821. Unusual celebration is in order, Sally." He nodded to his sons. "Stephen, David, go to the barn and find the box in the feed room. It contains a complete set of pink and white dishes, the Willow pattern. Unpack the china carefully. We shall use it for dinner and supper. Perhaps our neighbors will be dropping in during the afternoon. If so, I want them to realize how proud we are, how happy. Everyone must know that we rejoice at the safe arrival of our most precious Christmas present."

"*What* present?" Sally was ten—and bewildered. All morning she had been conscious of a suppressed excitement in the air, a tension she felt and could not understand. And as for people dropping in: already the doctor had come, lumbering in his carriage the difficult miles from Worcester. Sally had thought a great deal about the doctor's visit. Could he have had some treasure hidden in his old brown satchel? "What *is* it, Father?"

"I shall show you." He went quickly out; they heard his footfalls, the click of a doorknob, a faint, queer cry. Then he was back again, in his arms a compact, blanket-swathed bundle.

"Oh," shrilled Sally, "a kitten!"

"No, not a kitten." As they crowded about him, Sally on tiptoe, tall Dorothy and the husky boys at his elbow, Mr. Barton drew aside a corner of the blanket.

"A baby!" Sally's eyes were round with astonishment. "For mercy's sake, a *baby!* Is it a sister?"

"Yes, a sister."

"Can we *keep* it?"

"Don't say 'it,'" Dorothy admonished, looking down at the little wrinkled countenance beneath the fuzz of dusky hair. "Say 'her'—and, of course, we'll keep her, and love her very much!"

"I suppose she's all right, isn't she?" Stephen's anxious gaze sought his father's. "I mean, sir, it's natural she should be so tiny?"

"And so awfully *red?*" David queried.

"Quite natural."

"Newborn babies are always tiny and red," Dorothy asserted scornfully. "Wasn't Sally like that?"

"The boys have forgotten what Sally was like when she was only an hour old," Mr. Barton said. "Stephen was but five then, and David three. How could they remember? Why, you yourself were scarcely seven, daughter!"

"And yet I think I do recall it perfectly." Dorothy timidly touched the bundle. "I'm longing to hold her! May I, for a minute, please?"

"Tomorrow," Mr. Barton promised. "Each of you shall have a chance to become acquainted soon with Miss Clarissa Harlowe Barton—"

"Oh, beautiful!" Dorothy clapped her hands. "Mother has named her for Auntie, your sister, hasn't she? And also for the heroine of the novel by the English writer, Richardson?"

"Clarissa Harlowe Barton?" Stephen whistled. "A heavy load for a tyke to carry!"

"We needn't call her that," Sally said.

"I'm going to call her Clara." David tweaked at the edge of the blanket. "Hi, Clara! You can have Button, my puppy, for your very own." Suddenly a little fist, rosy and curved as a periwinkle shell, thrust out from the folds and waved vigorously. "Clara's strong!" David exclaimed. "A scrapper!"

"I expect she'll be stubborn," Stephen said. "We are all that." David chuckled. "Nobody can be as stubborn as a Barton."

"Will she be pretty?" Sally asked wistfully. "Because she isn't now—and I do wish she would be!"

"I think she'll probably resemble her mother, Sally," Mr. Barton said.

"Then we can count on her being pretty!"

"She's the most wonderful baby on earth!" Dorothy grasped the little clenched fist and gently lifted it to her cheek. "I pray she may have a wonderful life."

"God grant it! And," Mr. Barton added, "a useful life."

"The odd thing is," Stephen said, "that you can't tell at the beginning what any life will be. There's no way of telling or forecasting."

"No way at all, my son." Mr. Barton shook his head. "But this child begins her mortal pilgrimage on the best and holiest day of the year."

"And that may be an omen?"

"Perhaps." Smiling, Mr. Barton gathered the bundle closer. "Who knows whether the greatest of destinies is not in store for her? *Who knows?*"

2

To THE little girl growing up in it, the hillcrest farmhouse seemed to contain all that she needed—shelter, warmth, substantial food and clothes, much affection. Though she lacked playmates of her own age, she was never lonely: Dorothy, Sally, and the boys were devoted to her; when they were not available for entertainment, Clara shadowed her busy father as he went about his duties. She watched and had a part in such chores as milking and churning and the planting of gardens. She weeded onion beds and picked the berries for pies. She liked to do things!

She was her father's sworn comrade and an eager listener to the stories he had to tell—about the Bartons, those earliest ones in old England, whose ancestry dated to the era of William the Conqueror, whose names were inscribed in the Domesday Book; and those who in 1640 had emigrated to become pioneers of New England, settling in Maine, New Hampshire, and Massachusetts.

Of the American Bartons certain figures stood out: Edward, the patriarch; Matthew, the sailor and shipbuilder; Samuel, the defender in Salem of persecuted men and women accused and often killed by the fanatic witch hunters. Samuel, in his zeal for tolerance, had married the niece of Rebecca Nourse, hanged as a witch on Salem Hill in 1692. After that tragedy he went with his wife to Framingham and later to Oxford,

7

a village then being founded on the former site of a Huguenot colony which the Indians had obliterated in a bloody massacre. It was from Samuel that Clara Barton's father was descended.

But no tales were so enthralling, Clara thought, as the ones of Father's own youthful experiences. He had been a soldier in the wars of the western frontiers. Under the command of Mad Anthony Wayne, beside William Henry Harrison and Richard M. Johnson, young Stephen Barton, a noncommissioned officer, had marched through the wilderness campaigns against the savage Indians. He had loved his country, served it well—and marched home at last to marry Sarah Stone in Massachusetts.

"Your mother," he said to Clara, "was a charming girl. A hot temper, a tender heart, and a level head. What more could a man seek in a wife? . . . Fine people, the Stones."

He did not speak of his prosperity or his thrift, the acres he had bought and cultivated, the modest fortune he was accumulating, or of how he had been moderator and selectman for the town of Oxford and its representative in the legislature. But he made no secret of his interest in public and military affairs and politics. He wanted Clara to understand and be interested, too.

In the long, lamplit evenings she would curl up on his lap while he recited the names of the President, the Vice-President, the members of the Cabinet.

"These are names you ought to know, Clara. Say them after me."

She said them, glibly, and tried to visualize how the great men must look. They'd surely be quite different from other folk, bigger; the Vice-President about the size of a barn, the President even larger. Somehow she fancied that the President (he was John Quincy Adams) might be painted green, though she couldn't have told why.

Her father drilled her in military etiquette, the relative stateliness of titles. "This may not seem important, Clara, but it is. Just address a captain as 'lieutenant' once and you'll find out! You might as well learn the dignity of rank in armies."

Sometimes they got down together on the floor and with bits of kindling and pebbles staged martial parades or sham battles. Then Mother, quiet in her chair beside the table, would smile over her knitting and say:

"I notice Andrew Jackson is always the leader of the winning army."

"A proper hero!" Father would retort. "Old Andy'll be President before he's through, mind what I say. And I'll have voted for him!"

He liked to see a crimson ribbon tied in Clara's thick dark hair or a splash of scarlet flowers pinned to her little gingham apron. "Red's the Barton color. Wear it whenever you can, daughter. A brave color!"

"And cheerful," Mother would say. "There! I'll just put a red thread into this muffler for you, dear."

She had no dolls (Mother thought they might be frivolous) or other toys, but she had dozens of animal pets. Whole families of cats were in the haymow, chickens and ducks in the fowlyard, cows with wobbly-kneed calves in the barnlot. Behind pasture bars grazed the pedigreed colts which Mr. Barton bred and sold: Highlanders, Morgans, and Virginians, with their fiery eyes, quivering nostrils, arched necks; equine aristocrats disdainful of the rough plow-horses moving complacently through fields beyond the fence.

Of all the living creatures, Clara most adored Button.

White and silky, alert for any lark, the terrier was always at her flying heels.

On weekdays, Clara seldom ventured past the meadow bounds. But every Sunday, rain or shine, she clambered over the wheel of the wagon to which a team had been hitched and, perched on the seat between her parents, she went to "meeting."

The Oxford Universalist Church claimed to be one of the earliest of its denomination in America or in the world, and the Bartons had helped to organize it: their funds and the work of their hands had contributed to the erecting of the original meetinghouse. Dissenting from the Congregational sect which they deemed too strict, the Universalists believed themselves to be extremely modern and liberal. Yet no heat was permitted in the church even in extremest winter weather.

There was that dreadful day when Clara heard the rambling, interminable sermon delivered by Hosea Ballou, the famed preacher, and felt her feet freezing numb in their small, tight boots.

At noon, slipping from the pew, she stumbled and fell in the aisle. She was apologetic. How disgracefully clumsy of her!

But her father was only angry. "Why didn't you say you were getting so cold? Why sit there and not a peep out of you? We wouldn't have stayed."

"We couldn't have interrupted the Reverend Mr. Ballou's discourse, Father."

"Indeed, we could! And next time we will!"

He was not sternly religious. No formality of conduct ever mattered so much to him as the comfort of his dear ones.

Clara was an active, healthy child with an amazing aptitude for remembering and plenty of opportunity to absorb information. Each of the sisters and brothers undertook some phase of her education. Dorothy taught her to read and spell. Teaching was Dorothy's profession. At seventeen she was in charge of a local school. And Sally taught Clara to write. ("Look, that's your signature." Patiently Sally guided the stubby fingers and firm-clutched pencil across a squeaking slate. " 'Clara Barton'—that's *you*.")

David's instruction was of a practical nature. He was hardy, athletic, expert with tools and at games. From him Clara learned to drive a nail straight, to tie a knot that would never unravel, and how to throw a ball and spin a top.

Horses were David's passion. He took Clara to the pasture and hoisted her up on the back of a mettlesome thoroughbred.

"Knowing how to ride is nothing more than knowing your mount, Sis. You must think of this Morgan as half of yourself."

"Of *myself*?" She glanced down from what seemed a perilous height.

"The bigger half, by far. But you're the brains of the combination, you're the one to give the orders, and you must make him *know* it. Here, grab the mane. Stick like a burr and we'll have a gallop."

"Oh, David, I—"

The protest was never concluded, for David had leaped astride a second colt. "Yip!" he yelled—and they were off, surging over the turf, rocketing through the orchard. Clara was utterly terrified, but she managed to cling to the Morgan's mane, she was not unseated.

When they had returned—and no mishaps, no spills—she queried breathlessly, "Was I all—all right, David?"

"You ride like a Mexican." He lifted her down and patted her head. "A born horsewoman!"

Stephen, the mathematician, initiated her into the mysteries of numbers. Once, to illustrate, he brought home an enormous cake of maple sugar which Clara must divide equally among the Bartons.

"Each of us is to have a piece," Stephen said. "How many pieces will that be?"

Father, Mother, Dorothy—"*Seven.*" (What a lovely lesson. How clever Stephen was to think of it!) Clara made seven wedges of the sugar cake.

"We'll line up against the wall," Stephen said. "You give us our portions and what's left is yours."

Gravely, for this was no trivial matter, Clara went along the line, parceling the sweet into the outstretched palms. And then she came to Button. He was waiting with the rest. And why not? Button Barton! He was fond of maple sugar. Clara laid the seventh piece on Button's paws—and he snapped it up, gulped, licked out his pink tongue. Clara laughed. It had been fun to see Button do that.

But in just a minute, "*I* haven't any," she wailed. "Where's *my* sugar?"

"If you meant for Button to share, your calculations were wrong. But, heavens, don't cry!" Stephen said, as tears welled in Clara's eyes and she opened her mouth ominously. "You can have my candy."

"She shall have *mine*," Dorothy said.

"The poor baby," said Father. "Here, Clara."

Sally and David rushed forward too; but Mother had other notions.

"No," she said. "We mustn't give back what she's just given us. She is a very little girl, yet not too little to think things through before she acts. She must be generous, but *sensible,* never robbing herself so that she's an object of pity to everyone else."

"Please, Mother," Stephen entreated. "I wouldn't make Clara cry for anything!"

"Nor I. And so," Mrs. Barton said, "we'll each break our candy into bits and have another and an equal division. Now, Clara, use your head, my dear."

Thus the problem was solved. Clara used her head—and had as many delicious morsels as she was entitled to.

Only Button did nothing at all about the reapportionment. He didn't bark remorse or ask pardon or even look guilty. He just licked his chops and wagged his tail.

For weeks, Clara marveled at Button's nonchalance in her dilemma. She loved him so much—and he was such a greedy, conscienceless sinner!

IT WAS the winter of 1824 and Clara, not quite four years old, was entering school.

Stephen carried her on his shoulders through the mile of snow and blustering wind, while David and Sally raced on in front, shouting and swinging their lunchboxes. Beneath her little beaver tippet, Clara's heart hammered at her ribs. School! What would it be like? She was hushed and wondering, shivering in the frigid air.

When the schoolhouse loomed in view, David and Sally sprinted toward it and disappeared through the door. Stephen proceeded more deliberately. In the diminutive vestibule, where the wraps were hung on pegs, he set his burden down.

"You must look neat, Clara," he said, and helped her out of cloak and bonnet, and smoothed her plaited hair.

There was no one else in the vestibule. "Stephen?"

"Yes?"

"I—I can't," she whispered above the subdued hum of voices from the next room. "I can't!"

"What's the matter? Are you scared?"

"I feel the way I did last summer when I chased the bird."

"And it turned into a snake?" Stephen remembered that incident: Clara's following the swift rippling of the meadow grass ("Oh, a baby robin!"), and then her scream as the quarry, clearly seen, was not a bird at all but a horrid, hissing serpent! Stephen had clubbed the snake and he and David had laughed. But Clara hadn't laughed. Sometimes in the night she dreamed of the coiled and writhing monster and woke, sweating, and had to scamper into Mother's bed and there be comforted.

Stephen squatted so that his eyes were even with hers. "It's only natural you should feel rather queer, your first day away from home." He grasped her arms. "But you're not afraid."

"I am. I *am.*"

"Well, if you really are—then you haven't any choice, have you?"

"Why—why not?"

"Because the thing you're scared of is the thing you must do." Coaxingly he kissed her cheek. "Face up to it, Clara. Sally and David and I are here with you. Think of us, and of Mother and Father. Make us proud of you."

Her brown gaze contemplated that, the vision of herself making them proud. And she sighed. "All right," she said, and let Stephen lead her in.

It was a little schoolroom, very crowded with benches, desks and stools, and with people; boys and girls of all sizes, even a few young men and women who, like Stephen, were acquiring the education to become teachers themselves. This was a superior school, and Colonel Richard Stone, the master, was popular in Worcester County.

The bell hadn't yet been rung. No one seemed to heed Clara; she crept up on a bench and crouched, rigid with shyness, her feet dangling inches from the floor. The glimpses she had of Sally and her brothers mingling and chatting with the older pupils was somewhat reassuring, but she didn't dare look around her. Colonel Stone was at his desk. She could see him, with stacked books beside him and, at his elbow, a revolving globe on a pedestal. Behind, on the wall, was a blackboard with a ledge beneath for chalk and the ferule.

Presently Colonel Stone clattered the bell and the noise subsided.

"I think we may begin," the master said, as the pupils took their seats. "I shall not call the roll, for I recognize most of you. You've been here before. However"—he paused, glancing over his assemblage—"I shall ask the few newcomers to identify themselves. The little girl on the fourth bench. The one with the red ribbon. Stand down, please."

Clara gasped. That hateful red ribbon! Because of it, she had been singled out, Colonel Stone was speaking to *her*. Her heart shriveled. But there was nothing to do except wriggle off the bench and "stand down."

"Your name?"

She just managed it. "Clara Barton."

"Oh, yes." Colonel Stone nodded. "I hope you'll be as good a student as your sisters and brothers have been. Do you know the alphabet, Clara?"

"Yes, sir." She said it primly, struggling against a tendency to lisp. Sally was always giggling at Clara's lisp. How awful it would be if she were laughed at now.

"You will recite with the primer class," Colonel Stone said. "Come forward. Take this spelling book. Can you spell the words at the top of the first page. *At, bat, cat,* and so on?"

Clara took the book, stared at the page, and was silent.

"Well?" prompted Colonel Stone. "Well, Clara?"

Suddenly her chin jutted. "I can—but I won't."

"What did you say?" He was obviously startled.

"I won't, sir." She had never been so frightened, but she

was offended too. *At, bat, cat!* The very idea! "That isn't where I spell, sir. I spell in *artichoke*."

"Why, that's the lesson for the third grade."

"I spell in *artichoke*," she repeated firmly.

Colonel Stone frowned, his handsome chin whiskers quivered, and then he smiled. Someone in the rear of the room tittered. And then they were all laughing, and it *was* awful. She flushed miserably. What had she done but tell the truth?

Colonel Stone seemed to sense her chagrin. "I've underestimated you, Clara," he said. "Yes, you belong with the advanced pupils."

As she trudged back to her seat, a little girl at a near-by desk plucked at her sleeve.

"I wish *I* could spell in *artichoke*." The little girl was Nancy Fitts, plump and blonde. "You're smart! Let's be friends, shall we?"

At the noon recess they ate their lunch together, Clara and Nancy Fitts. They traded a red apple for a bunch of raisins— and they were friends.

Nancy was five, but this was her first year at school too. "It's fun," she said. "I'm going to love it."

"It isn't so bad," Clara said. "I'll never love being anywhere but at home, though. I'm afraid of strangers."

Though she might shrink from the "strangers," Clara liked the reading, writing, and arithmetic of school. And the geography—that best of all! She was fascinated by Colonel Stone's revolving globe and by the maps. Rivers and mountains and plateaus; towns and cities; lands beyond the seas. Would she ever journey to any of them? Probably not. But she could imagine such journeyings, could pore over the charts and picture herself on far continents, Europe, Asia, Africa, in jungles and deserts, on ocean expanses.

For Christmas her father gave her a copy of Menseur's *Geography and Atlas.* Nothing, not even the cage of yellow canaries which was Stephen's gift, could compare with that possession.

Sally said that Clara was getting to be a nuisance. "She's running the geography business into the ground." And Sally had reason for complaint, for often she was roused during the night by Clara, sitting erect beside her in the bed, with Menseur's volume spread open on her knees and the candle lighted on the window sill, shedding a fan of mellow luminance.

"Sally. Hey, Sally!"

"What on earth?"

"Where's Cape Horn?"

"Oh, fiddlesticks!" Sally would blink up rebelliously from her pillow.

"I can't find it. And I have to! Where's Cape Horn?"

For a minute Sally would fume, and then, "Oh, it's *there*," she'd say.

"Why it *is,* isn't it?"

"And now will you go to sleep like a civilized child? Or shall I tell Mother?"

But having located Cape Horn, or the Sahara, or the Bay of Biscay, or whatever thing which had eluded her, Clara was ready for sleep. "Thank you, Sally dear. I was so worried."

"Um—mm," Sally would grumble, and snuff the candle.

In January, Stephen was appointed as instructor in a school in the neighboring county. Clara missed him. But David said he would be her steed and carry her through the banked snow, up and over the hill to school each morning. Sally frequently preferred the society of her own classmates. As spring approached, David and Clara were more and more left to themselves.

David was seventeen, yet he had the tact to make his little sister forget the difference in their ages. He talked long and confidentially with her. Perhaps to a greater extent than anyone else, he tried to understand her timidity and to help her overcome it.

"You're a funny kid," he said once, when they had stopped in the pasture for a gallop on the evening way home. "A combination of lion and mouse." They had dismounted, he was locking the gate on the colts. "Riding, you never seem to have an ounce of fear—and many an adult wouldn't tackle these wicked fellows. But when Colonel Stone asks you to read aloud, you tremble like a leaf. And remember the day the folks went to the funeral in Webster? Mother said I was to stay with you—"

"You didn't though. You ran out of the house."

"Yes. The sky clouded over and I knew a storm was coming. I had to shut the barn doors. When I got back, you were down behind a chair—simply *squawking*. Why was that, Clara?"

"The clouds. They were shaped like that old ram, the ugly one Father had to kill because he was so mean. They *were* rams."

"They were clouds," David said. "You're silly!"

"I guess I am, David," she admitted penitently. "I guess I'm a coward."

"Well, *quit* being. You don't have to be anything you don't want to be."

"Really?"

"Of course not. You think too much about yourself, Clara, and what might happen to you. That's no way to live, all to yourself. Think about other people."

"I'll try."

"That's the ticket! But be independent, too."

"I will, David." She would do anything he advised.

Clara wished that this association might continue forever; but in the planting season, David was needed for farm work. At the same time, Sally was named as substitute teacher in town. Thus, with the commencing of the district school's summer semester, Clara was bereft of companionship.

It was then that Button proved his worth. Clara trained him to walk with her, carrying her lunchbox in his teeth. Occasionally he would dash off at a tangent, after a rabbit or a cabbage butterfly, but his behavior was usually admirable. He would go to the very door of the schoolhouse, halt there while Clara bade him good-by, then trot off with a parting flick of his tail and the manner of having performed a duty—and performed it nobly. In the afternoon, when school was dismissed, he would be waiting.

On the return trip, Button had two little girls to guard and pilot—anyway, as far as the fork in the road. Happily, their arms entwined, Clara and Nancy Fitts strolled under the full-blown elms and maples. At a certain spot they would stop and feed Button the remnants from their lunchboxes.

This was the high point of Button's day.

When she was five and completing her second year of school, Clara was desperately sick.

She retained only a misty memory of the excitement she caused—of David's hasty saddling of Black Stallion, the king of the colts, and thundering down the lane to fetch the doctor from Oxford five miles away; of her family's stricken faces and their fervent prayers. When she floated back to consciousness, it was to find herself propped up in a huge cradle which long ago had been carved out of a log as a bed for some adult invalid. She was hungry—starving—and demanded food.

Dorothy brought her supper on a dainty tray. A two-inch cube of toasted rye bread, a midget glass of blackberry cordial, a bite of cheese.

"Is that *all?*"

"It's quite enough, Clara," her mother said. "Eat it slowly."

She made it last as long as possible, sipping and nibbling. Then she was instantly asleep and did not hear her mother say, "She'll soon be well," or her father's exclamation, "Praise God!"

4

Sıx months of school each year, six months of play—this was the pattern of existence, and very satisfactory, too. Clara supposed it always would be just so. Then she was eight, and the pattern abruptly shifted.

Colonel Stone went from the rural district to establish a large "high school" in Oxford; Stephen Barton was promoted to the Colonel's former position; Dorothy and Sally were teaching regularly; Father bought a new farm to which he would move in the autumn—and there was talk of Clara's being sent to boarding school.

"We want you to have the best education you can get, dear," Mother said. "The very best."

Had she been allowed a voice in this decision, Clara would have voted an unqualified *no*. What was education if it took you away from home? But once made, the ruling had its consoling aspects. "The school might be worse," she said to David. "What if they shipped me off to Boston? At Oxford I'll know one person, at least—Colonel Stone. Oh, David, what'll I do without my own folks?"

"You'll get along," he told her. "Just don't be bashful."

On an April morning, Mother kissed her fondly and Father bundled her into the wagon and seated himself beside her. The weather was cold, no green showing in the treetops, the road still harsh and rutted with frost. Clara wore a fur-trimmed woolen mantle over her rose-sprigged challis frock; on her black hair (kept cropped since her illness of three years ago) was a velvet bonnet, the strings tied in a bowknot under her chin. Her hands were mittened; her stout little boots rested on the small leather dressing case which she called her "trunk" and which David had tucked under the laprobe.

The horses jogged, the wagon jolted; and Father and Clara, who ordinarily had so much to discuss, were almost entirely silent. Once Father commented on the thawing of the creek's edges, and for a while he whistled, rather drearily. At the fork in the road, Clara stood up to wave to Nancy Fitts, who was in the cottage window, flattening her nose against the pane. The rest of the drive was without event.

They were at Colonel Stone's house in time for dinner, and soon afterward Father took his leave. Then Clara knew, with a sinking sensation in her stomach, that she was adrift from everything dear and familiar.

There were a hundred and fifty pupils in the school, the majority of them day pupils. With Clara, there were fifteen boarders, more boys than girls, and she was the youngest of all. She met the other boarders that evening at supper in the hall, which seemed to Clara enormous and unattractive. She couldn't have told what any of the children looked like, she scarcely saw them; she couldn't eat the nourishing food on her plate. Homesick, solemn as a little owl, she said nothing —and wished for a magic deliverance which did not come.

At bedtime she reproached herself. How stodgy she'd been, bashful—though David had admonished her about that—and only because she'd thought of herself. Tomorrow she'd think of other people. To be brave, that was the Bartons' motto.

"I'll try," she vowed.

She did try. Next day and for many days she smiled brightly

at everyone until her jaws ached, swallowed the food put before her, never tasting it, concealed the pangs of yearning for home. And she felt much better. But then occurred that ill-starred history recitation.

Colonel Stone's pupils repeated their lessons by rote, a method which suited Clara very well, for she had an exceptionally quick and retentive memory. Her one perplexity was in the pronunciation of proper names, especially those of ancient Egyptian kings. Sometimes she didn't realize her mistakes until too late, as when she was asked to name a certain dynasty of Macedonian rulers. She rose, and said:

"Potlomy."

An instant of dead silence was broken by a guffaw from the corner of the room where the biggest boys sat.

"Potlomy!" someone cried and was answered by a derisive chorus springing up everywhere: "*Pot*-lomy!"

Clara reddened to the roots of her hair. This was quite like the day when she had said she spelled in *artichoke;* more dreadful, because then Sally and the brothers had been within reach. Now she hadn't an ally. Tears spilled on her hot cheeks; she wanted to die.

Colonel Stone had got to his feet; he pounded the desk. "Order!" And he said in an aside to Clara, "You may be excused."

She fled, the mocking chant wafting out and into the corridor, haunting her. "*Pot*-lomy! *Pot*-lomy!"

"I know they didn't mean any harm," she muttered to her reflection in the oval mirror above her bureau. "They'd have laughed at anybody else, just the same. And it *was* amusing."

She mopped at her tears and sat down with pen and copybook at the window. To show that a little thing like this couldn't disturb her, she'd practice her writing lesson.

The practice sentence was, "Man was made to mourn." And how true! "Man was made to mourn." She wrote it slowly.

Somehow the weeks went by. It was summer, a Sunday afternoon, beautiful with sunshine. Clara had taken her Bible into the front yard where the grass was soft and green and the oak trees were canopies of emerald shade. The Sabbath's lull was on the village.

Before settling to her Scripture study, Clara gathered a nosegay of cinnamon roses which bloomed, so yellow and fragrant, in the arbor. How lovely they were. She thrust a spray of roses into her belt, another into her neckerchief.

"Clara?" Colonel Stone was standing in the house door. "Come here to me, Clara."

Fearfully she went. Had it been wrong to pick a bouquet? Would she be punished?

"Colonel Stone, I'm sorry—I didn't—"

"Never mind," he said, and ushered her into the hall and upstairs, along a passage, into his library on the third floor.

"How do you do, Clarissa." A man who had been sitting in an armchair got up to greet her.

"Mr. Chandler!" She knew him well, the pastor of the Oxford Universalist Church, the Bartons' own pastor and an old friend. But why should he be calling now upon Colonel Stone? Had he come to scold her? Would they both scold her?

She was bewildered, and more so when Mr. Chandler politely shook her limp hand, when Colonel Stone said, "I want you to read for our guest." He got a book from a shelf; it was Campbell's *Pleasures of Hope*. "These lines." He indicated the page.

She put down the roses, took up the book, and read, " 'Unfading hope, when life's last embers burn' ..."

Colonel Stone did not interrupt, and she read on, the entire page, several pages. Finally he said, "That will be enough, Clara."

"It was nice," the Reverend Mr. Chandler said. "Very nice. And are you happy, my child?"

She looked apprehensively at Colonel Stone, dreading to hurt his feelings, but knowing she must not utter a falsehood. "I suppose," she said carefully, "I am as happy here as I'd be anywhere except at home."

"You are—thinner." Mr. Chandler spoke critically yet not unkindly. "Pale." He glanced at Colonel Stone, nodded.

"You may return to the yard now, Clara," Colonel Stone said.

She curtsied and went out. What a queer half-an-hour it had been. No rebuke, no word about the evil of picking someone else's flowers. Just the reading and Mr. Chandler's comment that she was thin and pale. All afternoon she wondered about it, and that night. But then she forgot. Probably it was only one of those happenings which are never explained, which really have no meaning.

Another Sunday, a week later, and she was in the yard again, and seeing the wagon trundling up the street. Something about the wagon, the look of it and of the team, made her breath quicken. Could it be—?

She darted to the sidewalk, straining her eyes. Oh, it was! It couldn't be—and it was!

The wagon came closer, stopped. Those men, they were Stephen and David; tall, brawny, bareheaded, in shirt sleeves, powdered with dust, grinning. Stephen jumped down and threw his arms around her, hugged her. David jumped down, seized her and tossed her high, almost to the sky. And why were they in town?

"Why? To fetch you home, of course," Stephen said.

"Pack your duds," ordered David.

In less than an hour they were starting for the country, the farm—home!

"Father and Mother never intended for you to be unhappy, Clara," Stephen said. "They didn't know, until Mr. Chandler reported, that you had no appetite, weren't eating or sleeping enough."

"I didn't tell Mr. Chandler that!" she cried indignantly.

"No. The Colonel told him. But Mr. Chandler saw you and confirmed Stone's opinion, that you ought to be at home."

David drove fast and recklessly, as he always did, and Clara felt like singing. She had a rough little voice without much music in it. But now it was charged with pure joy. She sang—and paused.

"I would have stayed." She laid a hand on Stephen's knee, a hand on David's. "I'd have faced up to it and been independent and not a coward. All the things you said. I meant to, honestly. But, goodness, I'm glad I didn't have to!"

There had been many changes during her absence.

The preliminaries for moving to the new farm were in progress. The house there (it was immense and had been in pioneer times a Huguenot stronghold against the Indians) would have to be repainted and repapered. Already it had occupants, the widow and four children of Father's favorite nephew, Jeremiah Larned; and Lovett Stimpson, the orphaned son of parents who had been friends of the Bartons. Father was a man who acknowledged the obligations of kinship and friendship. He was prosperous and he believed in being generous. He would provide for all the Larneds and the Stimpson lad until they could provide for themselves—and do it well.

"But, Father," Clara said, "the house isn't *that* roomy. Seven of us and—"

"The boys are remaining in this homestead."

She felt as if he spoke in riddles. "Stephen and David?"

Smiling, Father told her how the two young men had purchased the original acreage from him. They had bought other property too, a sawmill which they hoped to operate with profit.

"We'll keep bachelor lodge," Stephen said, "and when Dorothy and Sally are loafing between schools, they'll tidy up for us."

"The girls will be with you?"

"We hope so. Though," David said, "Sally has got herself a beau and she may elope."

"*Elope?*" shrieked Clara.

"Oh, hush, David!" said Sally. "You're always poking your nose into other people's affairs."

"But what about *me?*" After all, this was the thing which most concerned Clara.

"You'll live in both places," Stephen said. "A pity you're not twins."

"Let's divide her in two," said David, "as Solomon did the baby."

"Solomon didn't, though."

"You'll have to swear to split up your time evenly among us, Clara. Like the maple sugar. Remember?" said Dorothy mischievously.

"A fine arrangement," Stephen asserted, "and you'll think so, once you're accustomed to it."

Surprising how soon she was accustomed to it! And with

what speed she could scamper across the fields that intervened, with Button barking and frolicking beside her. At first she slept every night in the old house and worked by day at the new.

Father had engaged Mr. Sylvanus Harris to make the improvements in the Larned residence. Mr. Harris was the town clerk of Oxford, but the duties of his office being light, he plied the trade in which he had been skilled before his election. No one in the county could paint or hang paper so artistically and precisely as could Mr. Harris. Moreover, he was a genial gentleman and not averse (as Clara made it a point to ascertain) to having an assistant. He demonstrated for her the trick of mixing paint—and what a trick it was! The boiling of oil, the grinding and blending of dyes, the stirring, with a pinch of that added, a tincture of that, until the exact shade was there in the paint pot. When it was just to his liking, he gave Clara a brush.

"Swish it on," he said.

She started with the exterior walls (where, as Mr. Harris explained, "the daubs will never show"); then as she became more apt, she was allowed to finish the frames of doors and windows. For a week, they painted, Mr. Harris and his apprentice, side by side, as agreeably and cozily as could be. Only one thing marred Clara's bliss—and that not much. She was ruining her dresses, all her clothes were splotched and spattered. But for this David had a remedy.

One day he inspected the painting project. "That's it, Mr. Harris," he said. "Keep the young 'un busy. Put her through her paces."

"I'm as busy," Clara said, "as a cranberry merchant!"

"You look like a spotted coach dog." David laughed. "Haven't you a more appropriate outfit than that? Tell you what: tomorrow I'll bring you a pair of my overalls. You can roll up the pants legs."

At the end of the week, Mr. Harris went indoors—and Clara with him. Now there was putty to be mixed, and plaster, and various sorts of dryings, and bucketfuls of paste. The paper must be stretched out on the long measuring board, neatly sheared, smeared with the sticky, odd-smelling paste, slapped smoothly into line, with attention to the matching of seams.

Mr. Harris said it was best to work from the top of the house downward. And so he did, bedrooms and closets, upper passages, the stairwell, then the steep descent to the lower floor. On and on they papered, with the kitchen as the grand finale, where Mr. Harris even papered the cupboard shelves and got out his paint cans again and varnished the wainscot and the chairs.

A glorious month and it was over, the job complete.

At dusk on the last day, Mr. Harris cleansed his brushes in turpentine, stacked rubbish into a heap and set fire to it, stowed his tools in his bag, clasped Clara's grimy little paw in his big fingers and said farewell. She watched him go down the garden path. She was sad, with the feeling of emptiness. At the turn in the path he paused.

"Good-by, young lady."

She was on the verge of weeping. She had been so fond of Mr. Harris—and now he had gone. Of course, she could see him whenever she was in town. He had told her to visit him at the clerk's office. But that would not be the same.

She wandered into the house. It was immaculate; it glistened like a new pin. And there Clara's melancholy evaporated. She went from room to room. Every one was resplendent beyond description, perfect. And not one which she hadn't worked in!

She had explored the mysteries of paint and paper and knew them all. Her thumbs were sore, her knuckles calloused—and the house was hers, her very own, and would be, always.

That night when she was back with the family in the old hillcrest dwelling and had eaten her supper and undressed, she spied a box on the toilet stand beside her bed. It was a jeweler's box. She opened it. Inside, on a nest of cotton, reposed a small heart-shaped gold locket; underneath was a card: To A FAITHFUL WORKER—those words and many curlicues.

For her? But who was the giver?

Tripping over her trailing nightgown, she rushed into the sitting room.

"Maybe Saint Nick left it," Stephen said.

"Oh, Stephen! I'm not a baby. And it isn't Christmas."

"A fairy?" Dorothy suggested.

"A gypsy prince," David said dramatically. "A pirate, with a huge mustache and a patch over one eye."

"Crazy!" She looked at her mother. "Was it Mr. Harris, Mother?"

"I don't know," Mother said. "I really don't know, dear."

Clara never knew, either.

5

WHETHER or not the pretty locket could have been traced to him, Clara hadn't seen the last of Mr. Sylvanus Harris. One morning in the next spring he appeared at the kitchen door, a basket on his arm.

"Duck eggs," he said. "Thirty of 'em. Reckon you could wheedle some of your ma's hens into hatching 'em for you, Clara?"

"Oh, Mr. Harris!" His thoughtfulness almost overwhelmed her. "They'll be lovely on the Round Pond. How soon—"

"About four weeks," said Mr. Harris wisely.

Circular as a saucer, shallow at the brink and deepening in the middle, the Round Pond lay just in front of the house, like a watery gem. And in a month, thirty downy ducklings had picked their way out of tinted shells to enhance it.

They were as sturdy a brood as ever paddled: yellow as butter, sometimes calmly floating, oftener whizzing after any fly or bug on the pond's surface or quacking defiance at their foster mothers, three Leghorn hens that ran madly about on dry land. Throughout the summer they swam as they pleased and were fat and arrogant; their voices waxed to such a clamor that, in the autumn, skeins of migratory wild ducks, flying over, would dip down inquisitively.

"To see what the fuss is about," Father said. "Clara, your pets are famous in the countryside."

"Funny pets. They never even look at me unless I have a handful of corn." She smiled. "But they are rather sweet."

Those were happy seasons for Clara. She had never before been in constant contact with children of her own age. Now she was one of a noisy, romping group and days were not long enough for all their enterprises. The Larned boys and girls, Lovett Stimpson, Clara—the six had literally miles of territorial domain; they ranged from Peaked Hill to the Flowed Swamp, from Rocky Hollow to Devil's Den. They crossed French River on a narrow, swaying log; they penetrated into the dark, sinister wood. At the sawmill they rode the saw carriage far out over the raceway, with the millstream swirling tempestuously thirty feet below. (A shuddery thing to do—and one which you must do because it *was* so shuddery.) They leaped from the beams of the barn to the floor and crowned as champion the child who could alight without a bump or bruise.

Mrs. Barton and the mother of the little Larneds said it was only by the Lord's mercy that all their necks weren't broken.

Even school was fun when you could go with five other pupils—and when Miss Susan Torrey was the teacher. Miss Susan was young and pretty; Clara loved her. More for Miss Susan's sake than for her own, Clara studied diligently, and was "head" in the spelling bees and took the honors in history and arithmetic, and read the many books of classic literature which Miss Susan recommended, and wrote the prize-winning theme of the term.

Lovett Stimpson had a shock of corn-colored hair, a freckled face and a love for competition in any form. "Yah, yah, I can do something you can't do!" This was the challenge by which he lived. He could not always prove the statement. Clara was his equal in most sports; she could climb a tree faster and higher, and swing a cider keg to her shoulder with better grace. But Lovett could skate, gliding on steel runners over the Round Pond, which winter iced so evenly. Clara never learned to skate.

She had asked for a pair of skates for Christmas and been denied.

"Unseemly exercise for a girl," Mother said.

"Dangerous, too," said Father.

But every night Lovett skimmed and curvetted on the frozen pond, whistling enticingly at Clara in her bedroom window. Too enticingly! . . . One night she stole down the back stairs and out.

"Lend me your skates, Lovett."

Wonder of wonders, he had borrowed an extra pair, as if he had known she must succumb to temptation. They didn't fit. Not *quite*. But Lovett said they would do. He strapped them to her shoes, looped his wool muffler about her waist, holding one end in his hand.

"Come on! Like *this*." He struck off.

Clara thumped and staggered after him. There were ridges where the ice had cracked; he skipped nimbly over them. "Oh, wait, Lovett!" she screamed. "Wait!" His speed did not slacken, and Clara hit the ridges full force, her feet shot out from under her and she was down in a heap and being dragged along like a fettered calf to the branding pen.

"I've hurt myself! Lovett, I'm—*killed!*"

That stopped him. He whirled and bent over her. "Oh, Clara!" Her stockings were in shreds, blood trickled over the ice. "Are you really hurt, Clara?" He was horrified and contrite.

"I'm dying," she said with dignity. "Take me into the house where I can die in bed."

They wound the muffler around her knees to stanch the blood, and somehow she got into the house and upstairs. Seen by lamplight, the gashes seemed deep. Lovett said he would call Mrs. Barton.

"Don't you dare!" Clara exclaimed.

"But what *will* you do?"

She was rather in a quandary as to that. "Anyway, I'll not tell a soul!"

At breakfast, Mother said, "Why are you walking so, Clara?"

"You're limping," Father said, "like a horse with the string halt."

Well, she mustn't limp. But at supper time there was more comment. Very casually she acknowledged that she had scratched her knees a bit. And next morning she couldn't walk at all.

The whole story came out as Mother soaked loose the improvised bandages. The doctor was summoned. He shook his head. "She'll have to stay off her feet for a fortnight or more. If those knees hadn't been neglected—"

She sobbed out her remorse. How wicked she was, to deceive her darling parents! And all for vanity, to show off before Lovett Stimpson. Skating? She didn't know the first thing about it.

"It was Sunday, too. The Sabbath, and I desecrated it! I'll cry for hours. Maybe my tears will wash away my sins."

She cried for ten minutes and then felt strangely normal. But when Mother carried the dinner tray to the chair (in which she must sit for a fortnight!) Clara's brown eyes swam with tears.

"Oh, Mother, I'm such a *villain*."

Mrs. Barton neither agreed nor disagreed. She said quietly, "I remember the day I rode my father's Indian pony, though I'd been cautioned not to. The pony threw me, of course, and I broke my wrist."

Clara gasped. *"You* were never disobedient, Mother?"

"Oh, frequently. Yes, I had an iron will—which you've inherited, I think."

"And you've turned out so well! Maybe there's hope for me."

"I shouldn't wonder. If you'll not foolishly repeat your blunders."

"No," Clara vowed. "I won't."

A consequence of the skating accident was that Clara and Mother drew together into a closer bond of understanding.

"I've seldom been alone with you, dear," Mother said. "When you were a little tot, it was as if you had six parents instead of the usual two, and the other five were wanting to teach you things."

"And hadn't you anything to teach me, Mother?"

"Perhaps." Mrs. Barton smiled. "But I've just bided my time. I knew that sooner or later you and I would have the opportunity really to get acquainted."

Now they got acquainted, Clara and Mother. During the day they had the house to themselves, for Father was in the barn or in the village, the other children were at school, and Mrs. Larned had temporary work somewhere as a seamstress. With the winter weather shutting them in, shutting visitors out, they sat beside the hearth, snug and warm.

And how delightful it was! Clara read aloud, *Arabian Nights,* from cover to cover, pausing occasionally to munch a red apple or a handful of popcorn from the blue bowl on the table, while Mother placidly knitted. Clara learned to knit, too, and to baste and hem and stitch the garments which Mother was sewing for poor families in the community. Mother had always at least a dozen needy people for whom she planned and worked. Her charities were unobtrusive but genuine. She looked well to the conduct of her own household, and then she looked beyond to other, less fortunate households. And she could do anything with a needle.

Indeed, Clara had not properly appreciated Mother or her accomplishments. "You're so clever, Mother."

"Clever? Oh, no. Why, I'm just a typical New England housewife."

"It's a fine thing to be," said Clara.

She started a sampler, like one which Mrs. Barton had made when she was just a girl. With blue and pink and purple floss, Clara embroidered on coarse netting the eternal verity: *Virtue is its own reward.*

"And you might memorize that," Mother said. "It's worth remembering, I think."

"I will," said Clara dutifully.

When the knees had healed a little, she hobbled after Mother into the kitchen. Mother was an expert cook. Thrice each week she baked; the whole house would be suffused with the heavenly odors of frothy yeast, loaves browning richly in the oven, sugar melting to caramel, cinnamon and molasses. Clara learned to knead the dough and pat it into rolls and twirl symmetrical figure eights of coffee cake. One day she made a pie; the crust was crinkled, the filling a creamy custard.

"You're an energetic piece," Mother said. "Like a clock. You've got to be wound up and ticking; when you run down, you're good for nothing. You can't abide idleness, can you? Well, I've always been a worker, myself."

Skating was not the only exercise forbidden Clara.

In May of that year, a foreign gentleman came to Oxford, where he would have a dancing class, instructing the young folk in the minuet, the lively waltz, and elegant ballroom deportment.

"May I join the class, Mother?" Clara asked. "Please Father, may I?"

They were at supper when the question was raised. Stephen was there. He had strolled over from the old farm and was seated across the table from Clara.

"Dancing?" Mother said. "I think not."

"No," Father said, and added, "Not that I disapprove of the diversion. I don't. But so many of our fellow church members are against it. They would be scandalized if I permitted you to dance in public."

Stephen took no part in the conversation, but his straight-set lips and furrowed brow were austere, and when Clara got up and went out of the room, he followed her.

She was standing at the pasture fence. The night was vast, with moonlight draped like a silver shawl on tree and bush. A colt nuzzled toward her, snuffling with soft nostrils at her sleeve. She stretched her arms around its neck and felt its hoarse breath on her cheek.

"Clara?"

"Oh, is it you, Stephen?"

"I think you should dance if you want to. Scandalized church members! I don't care one whit about them."

"It doesn't matter. Why, it's nothing."

"You're disappointed. And I'm going to make it up to you, some way. David and I will. You'll see!"

Stephen and David . . . She thought that with such brothers she was surely the luckiest girl in the world.

The disappointment was sponged from memory as though it had never been, for Olivia Bruce, a schoolmate, had a party.

The date was "Old Election Day" and Clara went with Nancy Fitts. It was a "dress up" party; each guest must wear a particular kind of apron over her frock. The aprons were ordered from the village store, and they were so beautiful they dazzled you. Squares of snowy lawn stamped with green vines and plump brown birds! The thirteen girls, in their aprons and all with sashes of blue ribbon and blue bows in their hair, were as much alike as they could make themselves.

They played games; "Chase the Squirrel," "Hunt the Slipper," and "Farmer Jones":

> "The needle's eye that can supply
> The thread that runs so truly.
> For no man knows
> Where oats, peas, beans, or *barley* grows."

And at five o'clock they had tea and cakes and peppermints and cherry tarts. They went home by the setting sun.

"Were you good, Clara?" Mother queried. "Did you mind your *p*'s and *q*'s?"

"I hope so," she said. "I ate a lot. The food was *sumptuous.*"

David Barton had his father's honesty, shrewdness, and industry. Forever bent on developing his farm property, he determined to build a new barn. It would be an uncommonly capacious one, the biggest in the county, and to get the labor well under way, he would have a "raising."

He had dug his cellar (this in itself would mark David's barn as unusual) and had hauled timber to the site. When the day for the raising dawned, brisk and bright with summer sun, the lanes for miles around were dotted with people hurrying toward the hillcrest. The men carried axes and hatchets; the women and children lugged hampers of preserved fruit, pickles, and jam. Of course, Mrs. Barton and David's sisters would have prepared a bounteous meal, but a barn raising, the hours in the open, always made everybody ravenously hungry.

Nothing, as Clara was afterward to remember, could have been more auspicious than the day's beginning. The men joked and laughed. The earth seemed to echo and shake with the blows of their hammers, the whine of the saws. By noon the uprights had been set, the sheathing of the lower story nailed into place. Then David called, "Time for refreshments!" The women and girls spread the feast upon a table made of planks laid over long trestles—and there was everything you could think of to eat, even to baked beans from the huge stone jar which Mrs. Barton had been warming in the outdoor oven.

Clara presided over the milk jugs, passed out the glasses of foaming cider, and poured the coffee, still redolent and steaming, from the gigantic pots. When the men went back to the barn, it was midafternoon. Now they would attach the rafters to the ridgepole.

This was the feature of the occasion, and David would have the honor of fixing his own rafters. No one else could have done it so well, anyway. David Barton was an athlete, lithe as a willow sapling, strong as a bull. They all congregated to watch as he shinned up to that dizzy height and stepped out on the board which had been shoved over (and so very far above!) the yawning cavern of the cellar.

The board was none too steady, but David was sure of foot.

He walked to the center, balancing delicately, pausing to look down.

"Hello, Clara!" He saw her among the crowd. "Hi, Sis!"

Clara smiled. Wonderful David!

But the board on which he stood suddenly buckled, the two ends lifting from their supports, snapping like the blades of a jackknife closing. And David fell.

They pulled him up from the cellar's brick floor, and he insisted that he wasn't much damaged. It was only a tumble—and hadn't he landed on his feet? They prodded him for shattered bones, and there were none. His lips were rather pallid, but he grinned. He sat a minute under the trees. Presently he was swinging an ax with the best of them.

"Haven't knocked your innards out o' whack?" the men asked him.

"I'm fit as a fiddle," he said. "Just a slight pain behind my eyes. That'll wear off."

It did not wear off. For a month, day and night, it pulsed naggingly. And then it wasn't a slight pain, it was a torturing demon. One morning David didn't get up. Clara laid cold, wet cloths on his forehead and brought him sips of cool water.

"He's feverish," she said, when her father came to take her home to supper. "I'll stay with him."

Mr. Barton frowned. "If he isn't well tomorrow, I'll drive into town for the doctor."

Clara made a pallet for herself beside David's bed. He slept in snatches; she did not sleep at all. She would hear him threshing about, muttering.

"What is it, David?"

"You there, Sis? Fetch a drink, will you?"

The doctor said this was a "settled fever." It would run a

course of seven days and could be checked by blistering. He put mustard plasters on David's back and chest and left a bottle of pills. "Dose him with these, Clara."

She dosed him. The fever went up a degree. David drowsed and wakened to beg that the blistering be stopped.

The second doctor said that David had "too much blood." He prescribed bleeding, by cupping and by the application of leeches. "The fever will abate," he said, "in fourteen days—or twenty-one," and he left a bottle of powders.

Cringing, Clara placed the writhing, loathsome leeches on David's arms and ankles. His temperature soared.

In September the two doctors told Mr. Barton that his son was beyond medical or surgical treatment. Blistering, cupping, leeching, pills, powders, a dozen drugs, all had been tried, and the fever had not yielded. The doctors were beaten and admitted it and went sadly away.

"I don't believe them," Clara said passionately. "I won't."

In the late autumn, the fever broke of its own volition, David seemed to rally somewhat.

"But I'm weak as a kitten," he complained. "I can't lift my head from the pillow."

"You're going to be much better now, David," Clara said.

"Am I?" He smiled wanly at her. "Why aren't you in school?"

"I didn't want to go. Mother said I might stay with you until you're well."

"That may be a long time, youngster. The doctors never come any more, and I know why. They've given me up. Maybe everybody's given me up—but you."

"Oh, no, David. And I'll never give you up!"

"I'm so tired. Read to me, Clara. Recite some verses."

She read *Aesop's Fables, Pilgrim's Progress,* the Psalms, and the Proverbs. She recited poems, even inventing a few. He scarcely seemed to listen, but when she paused, he bade her go on. She washed his face and hands as if he were a baby, and fed him from a spoon. Weeks of that, months. It was winter, spring . . . summer.

The other members of the family hovered outside the sickroom door, but the sight of anyone else irritated David. He was fretful. He wanted only Clara. "You there, Sis?"

Once she had clung to him as a bulwark of muscle and nerve, now he needed her.

"Where *are* you?" he would moan in the dark night.

"Here, David."

She was always there.

Her mother was almost as distressed for the nurse as for the patient. Mr. Barton scoured the county for doctors. When a new one came, Mrs. Barton asked whether Clara should not be ·barred from this duty she had assumed. "The confinement is so bad for the child!" But the doctors replied that she seemed to have a soothing effect on the poor young man, and their dubious countenances said also that Clara's confinement wouldn't be prolonged indefinitely.

In the twilight of a crisp October day, while David napped, Clara crept out into the yard. The evening was tranquil, sumacs flamed in fence corners; the beeches were bronze, maples and elms sheer gold. In a lavender-streaked sky one star pricked through.

David's illness was of more than a year's duration. In all that weary time she had been away from him, out like this, only for a few scattered moments. One thought, one wish had obsessed her. "Dear God, don't let anything happen to David. Not *David*."

She heard her father's anxious voice behind her. "Is the boy resting? Is he better?"

She turned. "Father, I'm afraid. He's really not a particle better. Will he—?"

"No," Father said. "He won't. He's tough. We're all tough, Clara. The Bartons have an inner fiber. We can stand things. David will not die. I've just learned of a doctor—"

"Oh, those doctors! They only exhaust him."

"This one is different. A new method. I've sent for him. Clara, will you pray with me for David's cure?"

They were praying when, back in the doorway, somebody called: "Clara?" It was Dorothy. "He's asking for you."

Dr. Asa McCullum was the new man, different, with another method. He arrived, diagnosed the case, and took the patient to his sanitarium twenty miles away.

David improved. In three weeks he was out of bed. Three weeks more and he was coming home.

It was like someone returning from the tomb.

6

"THE fact is," Mother said, "that you're worse off now than David. He's robust, quite the same as ever, except for that ragged, stubbly beard which I do trust he'll trim. But you haven't grown an inch or put on a pound in two years. And you're like a hermit."

"I can't get used to seeing people. For so many months, I didn't see anyone."

"You've always been so, more or less. These people you shy from—they only want to ask about David's cure and compliment you for the way you tended him."

"I know." Clara nodded meekly, aware of her shortcomings.

"Even at church you're fidgety."

Clara sighed. She did not relish the reminder of her conduct on a recent Sunday. She had gone to church without her gloves. Actually, she owned no decent gloves; her old ones were all out at the fingers. Mrs. Barton had been shocked to see her daughter's bare hands—and more shocked at Clara's saying that the omission of gloves from a Sunday costume couldn't really matter. She hadn't wanted to inconvenience anybody with buying her a new pair. "Haven't you the grit to speak up for things which should rightfully be yours?" Mother had expostulated.

And Clara had blushed and mumbled and not known just what to answer.

45

She was, really, in a peculiar state of mind, attempting to adjust herself to a world which seemed to have altered radically. Certainly she wasn't so childish as to have expected the world to stand still during those months when she was isolated in a sickroom. Time and tide, people and things, they must go on. Yet their going on so swiftly muddled her.

Now Sally had married the beau about whom David had often teased her. Sally was Mrs. Vester Vassall and living in a home of her own. Stephen had acquired a satinet mill, one of the earliest factories in America to produce fine cloth. Stephen also was to be married, and he was erecting his house. The widowed Mrs. Larned had taken her children into Oxford, where, with permanent employment, she could sustain herself and them. Lovett Stimpson had gone to the home of relatives who would educate him.

"You'll have to catch up with the times," Father told Clara. "You're as far behind as Rip van Winkle, that fellow in Washington Irving's tale. Why, I'll wager you don't know who's President of the United States."

"I'll wager I do." She smiled at him. "Andrew Jackson. Re-elected."

"Correct!" Father chuckled. "Didn't I always say—"

Clara went back to school for the summer term and again the following winter. She had excellent teachers to whom she would ever be indebted. She studied history, language, English literature and composition, philosophy, chemistry, and Latin. But when she was out of the classroom, she was plagued by the urge to be busy, every minute occupied as it had been while she cared for a querulous invalid. She was constantly seeking pastimes. She wrote letters and kept a journal. She knit and crocheted. She made herself a hat out of field straw, braiding and stitching the wisps and fastening a red rose in the brim. Her first straw hat. She thought she would never have another so stylish.

Though these diversions were all worth while, her parents and sisters and brothers believed that she needed further recreation, and, individually, they set about to provide it. Sally and Dorothy suggested that a poetry club be formed. Hadn't Clara always reveled in reading poetry? On Sabbath afternoons and rainy evenings thereafter, the exclusive little club met and commenced its reading with *The Lady of the Lake*—and straightway the Barton girls were transported in fancy to the bonny braes of Scotland, where they plucked the heather and the broom, steered the skiff across Loch Katrine ("Saxon, I am Roderick Dhu!"), and trudged with lovely Ellen toward Sterling Tower and the court of James Fitz-James.

Father, the rugged outdoor man, gave Clara a Morgan horse. Mother ransacked the attic and brought out the silver-mounted Mexican sidesaddle which had been her own in youth. Clara rapturously received the stallion and named him Billy. She hugged Mother and said the sidesaddle was a thing of beauty, she would enjoy riding on it—though secretly she knew that she always would prefer to ride astride.

Stephen offered Clara a vacation berth as an accountant in the mill, at a small salary. The offer, accepted, had its unlooked for aftermath.

The mill was enchanting, Clara thought. Not the office where she had her desk and stool, but the floor where the looms stood and the machines buzzed and clashed as the weavers' deft fingers flung the shuttles through the taut web. She was scrupulous with the accounting, but every half hour that she could spare found her straying after Mr. McDonald, the overseer, observing the processes by which the light oiled wool was changed into smoothly shining satinet.

And soon she had an ambition. She wanted to weave.

She broached the subject at the supper table—and knew instantly that the ambition was doomed. Mother's startled glance, Father's frown, were evidence of their opposition.

"No, dear," Mother said. "It would not be proper."

"You've had no training," Father said.

Strangely enough, Stephen was present that night. How similar these circumstances, Stephen must have thought, to a happening of several years ago. He saw the clouding of Clara's brown eyes.

"Aren't you drawing the lines too tightly on the youngster?" Stephen queried. "What's so wrong about her wanting to weave cloth in my factory?"

Father and Mother looked at Stephen and at Clara and at each other. Was this mutiny?

"You forebade her to skate and then to dance," Stephen said. "I have been sorry Clara did not have the fun of both, but you were thinking of the conventions. Now she's asking to work. Who would be affronted by that?"

"The point is," said Father, "that girls and young women from sheltered homes should not have to toil at machines."

"No," Stephen said, "the point is, sir, that Clara is not happy unless she's exerting herself in some work she *likes* to do. As for training: Was she trained to nurse? Yet she did that for almost two years, and never was anybody so efficient. Why must we be hampered with what is or what isn't proper? Mere phrases, empty of meaning. The Bartons have been liberal in thought since our grandsire scoffed at witchcraft. For my part, I'm ready and willing to put Clara at a loom."

"The looms are high," said Mother. "Clara couldn't reach them."

"I'll arrange that."

Clara had been listening with interest and amazement. But as first her mother and then her father smiled, she knew that Stephen, so polite yet so unyielding, had prevailed. She got up and ran to him and kissed his cheek.

"Stephen, you darling!"

"There," he said. "I told you I would."

Next day a low platform was laid down before a pair of glossy new looms in the factory room, and one of the cleverest of Stephen's weavers delegated to drill the beginner. Mounting that platform, surveying the evenly threaded warp, the shuttles, knowing they were hers, Clara felt, as she afterward said, like a young princess stepping to her throne. Attentive and too excited to be weary, she stuck to her post until sunset. In the morning she was awake at dawn—"Champing at the bit," Father said—swallowing her breakfast, hastening to the factory. As she climbed the stairs, into the whirring, clacking tumult, Mr. McDonald touched his tasseled Scotch cap to her as to a person who belonged in just that time and place.

On Saturday the webs were cut from her looms, inspected, and judged as first quality. She scampered to Stephen to report her success. "I love weaving! I'll never stop!"

On Sunday, the satinet mill took fire and burned to the ground.

With David, Clara gazed at the smoking ruins. "Of course, it's your fault," he said.

"Mine? Oh, David!"

"You worked so fiendishly fast, the friction set the mill to blazing." But he laughed and she knew he was joking.

Stephen, sooty and smeared with ashes, came up to them. "It started in the picker room, in a pile of wool. Spontaneous combustion. The flames licked down the air shafts and belt holes and lapped up the oil, and were beyond control. I'll rebuild at once."

"Everybody," David said, "has experimented with you and now it's my turn. *I* have a job for you, Clara. You'll have to go to Maine to do it."

"To Maine!" This must be more of David's nonsense. "Why, how could I?"

"Clara, I'm about to get married."

"You, too? What on earth's the matter with this family!"

"You know the girl I've been writing to? Julia? She's up there in a Maine seacoast town. I'm going after her. Well, will you go with me? Hurry and tell me!"

She would go, and she would have to hurry, for David was leaving in just two weeks. Clara plunged into preparations: dresses to be remodeled, baggage to be purchased; toilet articles, handkerchiefs, all the odds and ends essential to traveling, to be assembled and packed. Before she realized it, she was on the train for Boston, surrounded by the gay party of young gentlemen and pretty girls whom David was taking to his wedding, and stopping in Boston overnight, sleeping in a hotel (think of that—a hotel!), and then transferring to the steamship which would bear her across a corner of the Atlantic Ocean, that turbulent sea whose waves swelled against the shores of other continents, whose maps and charts she had dreamed over in Menseur's *Geography*. White and glittering, this was a fairy ship, and hers was a charmed existence. Leaning against the deck rail, seeing the leagues of undulant green water, gulls flying over, and the sky an arch of hazy blue, she wished she might sail on and on forever.

But they arrived at their destination. And there, at Julia's home, were festivities—and a surprise for Clara. She was to be the bridesmaid. That was the job David had for her.

"Do you think I *can?*" she asked incredulously.

"I'm sure of it," Julia said. "I have your dress and slippers and everything." She linked her arm through David's. "We won't have the ceremony without you, Clara. I shall send David home desolate and unwed."

What a terrible threat! "I should hate to have you do that, Julia. I shall be frightened. But, well, I'll be the bridesmaid."

"Spoken like a Barton," cried David. "Brave girl."

7

CLARA had the mumps.

She was more disgruntled than ill. What a dismally juvenile disease to contract when you're fifteen and just about to put your hair in a chignon and lengthen your skirts and be a young lady!

She lay on the sofa in the hall. In the next room, Mother was talking to Mr. L. N. Fowler, who had come to Oxford to lecture. There was nothing remarkable in Mr. Fowler's being in the parlor. Men and women of note were always calling on Mother and Father. Every town has its house to which distinguished visitors seem naturally to gravitate, and the Bartons' was such a house. Clara had been introduced to Mr. Fowler and liked him. He was a phrenologist. By placing his hands on your head and running his fingers lightly over your scalp, Mr. Fowler could tell you what sort of person you were and prophesy your future. He had put his hands on Clara's head—before the mumps had made her too grotesque to be seen in company.

But she realized after a moment that what was being said in the parlor was remarkable indeed. It was about Clara herself.

"A very comely and intelligent-looking girl," Mr. Fowler was saying. "Her wavy brown hair, her brown eyes and regular features, the broad brow and firm chin, these signify a forceful personality."

("Ah!" thought Clara.)

"She is little in stature, and slender; but her manner of walking, somewhat like an Indian's tread, never stooping her shoulders, gives her the appearance of height. I would not say that she speaks musically, but her voice has gentleness and some sweet tones."

("Well!" Clara smiled.)

"Her chief weakness of character," went on Mr. Fowler, "is an excessive sensitiveness, a tendency to draw away from people."

"That's it," Mrs. Barton said. "When anyone she doesn't know is here, Clara just shuts up like a clam. You'd think she was deaf and dumb."

("Humph!" muttered the eavesdropper.)

"She may always have this retiring nature. In my opinion, she will never assert herself *for herself*. She will tolerate any abuse of her own rights and privileges. But for others she will be perfectly fearless."

"What shall we do for her?" Mrs. Barton asked. "Our only desire is that she get the most out of life and the talents she was born with."

"She should have responsibilities," Mr. Fowler said. "She will not falter under them. I believe that all her earthly days Clara will fight injustice, cruelty, and oppression, and that her happiness will be in the contending more than in any victory she may win." He paused. "I see her future as extraordinary and good. Whatever she undertakes, she'll never fail."

When the dialogue was over, and even when Mr. Fowler had gone, Clara lay on the sofa, thinking, rehearsing his words in memory. Often and utterly she'd been disgusted with herself—and especially now that the hateful mumps made her comical as a figure in a cartoon. She knew also (and alas!)

the truth of what Mother had said: she was absurdly timid with guests; probably many people thought she was a dummy. But Mr. Fowler had described her as another sort of person, a splendid person. *Very* splendid.

She listened again, for now Father was in the parlor.

"Stephen," Mother said, "I've been counseling with Mr. Fowler. He feels that as soon as she's old enough, Clara should have responsibilities."

"What kind?"

"Well, he suggested schoolteaching. But what annoys me is this: How much faith can we have in Mr. Fowler's prophecies?"

"My dear, phrenologists are not scientists," Father said. "I doubt that the size and shape of the human skull and the bumps on it are an index to the brain inside that skull, or that the soul can be deciphered, as Mr. Fowler professes to do. And yet he's a cut above other phrenologists; an educated man, something of a psychologist."

"His guess about Clara was uncannily accurate," Mother murmured. "If it *was* a guess."

"She might take the examinations, anyway," Father said. "Then in the spring I'll inquire around for a school. She'll be a young, inexperienced teacher, of course."

("She'll be a *good* teacher," breathed Clara in the hall. "And Mr. Fowler is a good prophet. . . . 'She'll never fail.' Hah!")

The school was in District Number 9, near Sally's home, where Clara was to board during the term. The instructor preceding Clara had resigned his position because the bigger boys among his pupils had locked him out of the schoolhouse for six consecutive days—which must have been vexing, to say the least. As she walked up the hill path through the dewy grass that May morning, Clara speculated what her own fate might be. She carried a parcel of books, including her Testament, a packet of lunch, and, in her pocket, the certificate of an examination passed with flying colors.

At the top of the hill she stopped to scan the schoolyard. No one was in sight. Vivid sunshine spread serenely over everything—and silence.

She went to the door, foreboding assailing her as she turned the knob. But the door was not locked. It swung open, and she saw her charges, forty boys and girls of ages varying from four to thirteen, rosy-cheeked faces in smiling, expectant rows.

They stood up and chanted in cheerful singsong, "Good *morning*, Miss *Barton*."

But on a bench near the window were four boys who did not join the chorus. They were big boys, taller than the new teacher and, she felt, older too. One of them had a sullen mouth. And when Clara had hung her hat and shawl in the closet and seated herself at the desk, this one whispered something to his cronies, at which they all nudged one another and tittered. Clara didn't know what he had said, and had no wish to know; it was sure to be something uncomplimentary.

There was a lull. The children were waiting for her to begin the session. And, with a sensation of panic, she knew that she must act quickly. Forty pairs of eyes were on her, and the four loungers at the window were winking and grimacing.

"You may all sit down now," she said, steeling herself against the awkward moment. "And *you* may rise."

"Me?" The leader of the four got up, displeased at being made conspicuous. "Me?"

"Yes, you. What is your name? Nate Jones? Well, Nate, I want you to read some verses from the Bible." She handed him her Testament opened to the Sermon on the Mount.

"Out loud?"

"Yes, so that we may all enjoy them." As slowly, and most reluctantly, Nate droned through the verses, Clara thought of what she must do next. She couldn't let the children guess how dismayed she was. "Now you may tell us, Nate," she said when he had plodded to the end of the page, "the meaning of our Saviour's admonition to 'love your enemies.'"

But Nate had no intention of continuing as the center of things. He scowled and said, "I don't know."

"Does someone else know?"

Several hands fluttered, and one so emphatically that Clara said, "The little girl in the pink-checked pinafore."

"I'm Emily." The pink-checked pinafore bobbed a curtsy. "And I think Jesus meant that you must be good to everybody, Miss Barton, and mustn't quarrel or make nobody feel bad— and I'm going to try."

"That's right, Emily." Clara shot a glance at Nate Jones. If only *he* would try! "A splendid explanation, and thank you."

Somehow then (Clara never could imagine just how it was) a vociferous debate was launched in the schoolroom, with forty young Christians interpreting the Sermon on the Mount. Clara gave them each a hearing. She became intensely interested, gauging from what they said the amount of their information and whether or not they would be brilliant scholars or dull. The atmosphere was warm and informal, and when the morning had gone, so had her uneasiness.

But Nate Jones had not thawed. It would take more than this to impress him.

She went to see what could be causing the hubbub in the yard. That was at noon on her third day as a schoolmistress.

If the yells now bursting forth were any indication, she had a ticklish situation before her. Would she be able to deal with it? Would she ever get the hang of a teacher's job?

The children were embroiled in a violent argument, with Nate Jones the prime troublemaker, as might have been expected. There was a horseshoe green. Nate had a game—

"But he won't let anybody play except his own chums, Miss Barton," said Edward Gates, a fifth-grade pupil. "And he plays all the time, himself. It isn't fair!"

"No," Clara said, "it isn't fair. And Nate has no right to decide who is to be in the game. You must each have your turn, even the littlest ones."

Her words might have been a thunderbolt for the effect they produced. Profound quiet fell over the schoolyard. Clara picked up the horseshoes—and slouching forward, big Nate Jones glared at her.

"I'm the boss here," he said.

"You are? Why?"

"Because I'm the best pitcher." Nate despised all teachers, and one so small and slender as this was simply not to be endured. "Go mind your own business!"

The other children gasped.

"This is my business." Clara's knees trembled under her flounced skirt, but her voice was steady. "If you really *were* the best pitcher—"

"Who's better?"

"Well, I am, for one."

"*You?*" Nate snorted. "Shucks!"

"I think I can beat you at horseshoes, at lots of games," Clara said. "Shall we have a test?"

"I'd lick you!"

"Let's see you do it, Nate. Come, we'll have a game of horseshoes, and whichever of us wins will be the custodian of the green for the whole term. If you're the winner, then I'll never interfere again. But if I win, then I make the rules hereafter. How's that for a bargain?"

Nate scuffed the gravel. He thought the bargain was absurd, and Miss Barton obviously insane. But he had prestige, and he couldn't risk forfeiting it.

"Oh, well," he growled scornfully.

The green was cleared, the gallery for the match lining up on either side. Clara granted her opponent the first pitch. But some latent courtesy made him brusquely refuse.

So she took her place, toed the mark, flexed her arm. She said a silent little prayer—for much was at stake, far more than one game of horseshoes. ("I can't fail, I *won't*.")

She pitched, and there was the clang of metal on metal. And somebody cried, "A ringer!"

It was a thrilling contest, the score was close, but Clara was the better player.

More than once she had to exhibit her prowess in the recess hours. At such times she thought gratefully of David and of Lovett Stimpson, for it was their coaching which made her rule supreme, outside the schoolroom as well as in.

And gradually Nate Jones was won over. Perhaps he would never be much of a scholar, but there was good in him and loyalty which he gave to Clara. She had hit upon the surest way of convincing him that she was not an unmitigated nuisance.

The county trustees came to District Number 9 on the last day of the term and conferred a badge upon Miss Barton and congratulated her on the discipline she had maintained. She hadn't had to suspend a pupil, or whip one, or rap any knuckles or switch any legs. "A fine record," said the trustees, beaming.

Miss Barton blushed and bowed. But she thought there was an error, somewhere. Discipline? She hadn't maintained it at all. She wouldn't have known how to. And it never had been necessary.

"They were such dear children," she said. "I learned as much from them as they learned from me. Maybe more."

Part Two

8

"I HAVE been teaching for fifteen years."

Having jotted the sentence on a page of her journal, Clara put down her pen and stared at it, as if questioningly. Fifteen? An unconscionable length of time. But when she added the year at District Number 9, the four years in other districts, and the ten years in her own North Oxford school (which she had founded, and Stephen and David had built for her), she knew that the sum was correct.

She had loved her profession. To her, teaching had been an exciting, even a dramatic, adventure. She had small patience with any teacher who felt otherwise. She had believed that she must give to her boys and girls not only information, the facts (often rather stuffy) which were between the covers of textbooks, but also and in greater degree a sense of the richness and variety of life, the immensity of the earth and its peoples, the ever-recurrent delights of nature. And never a day went by that she had not spoken to them of their American traditions and heritage, how precious are freedom's ideals, how dear the institutions of democratic government.

As in that first term, she had always learned much from her pupils. She had retained their friendship. Little Emily, Nate Jones, Edwin Gates, and hundreds like them were adults now, yet still in touch with Clara Barton. She had attended their weddings, visited in their homes, been sponsor at the christenings of their babies.

She was thirty and known throughout the state of Massachusetts as a successful and popular teacher.

But in the back of her mind, and more insistent recently, had been the conviction that her own education was inadequate. She had not lost the taste for study, or the urge to go forward. Nothing bored her so much as being static; nothing lured her like the challenge of far-off horizons. She was, and would always be, the "energetic piece" of her mother's description, the clock that is useless when it runs down.

In vacation periods she had worked in her brothers' mills as bookkeeper and had thriftily saved this money as well as her teacher's salary. And at last—

"I am going to Clinton, New York," she wrote in her journal, "to study in the Liberal Institute there."

Stephen drove her in a cutter to the station. Roads and pastures were white with snow, sleighbells jingled. Though it was not yet winter, the weather had been cold for weeks. Stephen seemed rather depressed.

"As superintendent of the county school, I can ill afford to spare you, Clara. You're one of the most competent of my employees." He smiled. "But the days of my ordering you about are past forever, aren't they?"

"Would you wish to have those old days back?" She patted his fur-gloved hand.

"I can't say that I would," Stephen replied. "No, I like my life as it is, the commonplace, humdrum present. And, candidly, I think you wouldn't either, Clara. You were such a tiny, shrinking creature. Well, you're still tiny, of course, scarcely up to my shoulder and thin as a lath. But now—how self-reliant!"

He kissed her affectionately and put her on the New York train. "Good-by, Clara. Luck!" Perhaps it occurred to him, as he watched the locomotive puff out from under the shed and glide into the distance, that with this departure his little sister made a crucial step from the environment in which she had been reared.

Three days later Clara was in Clinton and discovering, to her annoyance, that the Liberal Institute was moving into new quarters, there would be a short interval before the college reopened. She went to the tavern, the Clinton House, and engaged a room. The interval drew out for several weeks. Clara familiarized herself with the town and its historic landmarks: the mineral springs, the iron mines, and Hamilton College, which had been named for Alexander Hamilton, with a cornerstone laid by Baron von Steuben. Then on a raw, blustery day the Institute was ready and, with other young women, Clara went up the plank walk, through terraced snow, and registered as a student.

The brick building was starkly new, sparsely equipped, never sufficiently heated. The interior was not homelike, and no attempt was made toward a more cheerful atmosphere. But Miss Louise Barker, the president of the Institute, was a person of such wisdom and charm that her presence compensated for the school's dearth of physical comforts.

Clara had a little joke with Miss Barker—or was it Miss Barker having a joke at Clara's expense? Anyway, Clara did not tell the faculty at Clinton that she had been a teacher. What fun, she thought, to enter merely as another student, one who never had had previous apprenticeship. If she weren't asked point-blank, she'd never breathe a word about those fifteen years as a schoolmarm.

She was not asked. But many of the programs were elementary; and, as usual, Clara felt that time was a priceless commodity. Each morning she was knocking at Miss Barker's door, inquiring whether advanced courses couldn't be squeezed into her schedule. Could she be admitted to this or that extra class?

And finally Miss Barker said, "We have a few studies left. Maybe you'd better just register for them all, Miss Clara. Take what there are. And we'll not mention your diligence, ever."

It was never mentioned, Clara's thirst for all the work she could pile up for herself. Miss Barker never hinted that the schoolmarm's masquerade had been detected. But her smile was very knowing.

The year at Clinton was so pleasant that the tragedy it held seemed by contrast inordinately bleak. Back in Oxford, Mrs. Barton died. Clara's grief was one never to be quite assuaged, just as her memories of her mother were to be eternally cherished. There had been the deepest love between them. Perhaps as a child, Clara had taken her mother too much for granted, but, growing up, she had realized the true beauty of her character. "A typical New England housewife," so Mrs. Barton had called herself. "A fine thing to be," her daughter had said.

And so it was. Perhaps the finest thing of all to be, for who can estimate the contribution of such women to the world's progress? They are there, in the background, self-effacing, often unnoticed, but their virtue is the rock upon which the structure of the family is erected, and with the family, all that is best in a nation. Often and tenderly Clara would recall her mother's devotion and care, her little ways and whimsical, endearing mannerisms. Some of the mother's qualities would be manifested in her youngest daughter so long as Clara lived —vigilance, resourcefulness, humility, and simple habits, the flashing anger that must be restrained, the knack of "thinking through" to a reasoned conclusion.

One of Clara's friends at the Institute was Mary Norton. When the semester ended and diplomas were awarded, she went with Mary to Bordentown, New Jersey, to stay a week or two with the Norton family, and there the opportunity came to her to teach the winter term in the Bordentown school.

"And why not?" she thought. "I don't want to go home. I couldn't bear Oxford just yet—without Mother. I'll do it."

This was a subscription school, each pupil must pay a fee. The amount collected was the teacher's salary. And what a *small* school. Only six boys. But there were literally scores of children in the town. Clara saw them everywhere, idling on street corners, playing in the park. She thought they surely would be drifting into her classes. When they did not appear, she became curious.

She stopped an urchin of thirteen one day as he paddled in the gutter. "Why aren't you in school?"

He was barefooted and ragged, and not very polite. "You ort'er know, lady."

"But I don't." She sat down on the curbing beside him. "Tell me."

Startled, the boy stared at her. "You'll get your dress dirty. Well, it's the money."

"The tuition? You can't pay that? But there must be a free school somewhere."

"No, ma'am."

"No free school?" She was puzzled. "Would you go if there was one?"

"Maybe," he said noncommittally. "I might. If it didn't cost nothin'."

That night Clara was demanding of the Nortons, "Why hasn't Bordentown a public school like those in Massachusetts?"

The answer she received seemed inadequate and even absurd —that the townsfolk regarded a public school as fit only for "paupers," that the well-to-do residents considered free education not worth the having.

"And what do the poor people think of the situation?" she asked.

"I suppose they don't think at all," said Mary Norton. "It's too bad, really a shame. But the poor can't do anything about it. What could *anyone* do?"

"That's what I'm going to find out," Clara said.

In Worcester County (and certainly in one person's opinion) learning was a necessity, an absolute essential, like food and drink. It should be so in New Jersey, too!

Mr. Suydam was Bordentown's postmaster and also the chairman of the School Committee. A kindly soul, he tried to explain to the slender little woman who had called upon him at his office that the latter title was meaningless.

"The Committee doesn't function, Miss Barton, with regard to *public* education, in the exact sense of that word."

"It should," said Clara.

Mr. Suydam blinked. "I understand your surprise at seeing our streets thronged with hulking young ruffians who can't read or write."

"I'm not only surprised, I'm indignant."

"But, Miss Barton, these boys are renegades."

"No, they're just boys, like any others, like your own. Perhaps they will be renegades, if something isn't done to prevent it."

"You have an idea for saving them from that fate?" Mr. Suydam smiled indulgently and thought to himself that Miss Barton, in her pretty bonnet and fashionable cape, was after all a stranger in the community and should not intrude upon matters which did not concern her.

"I intend to establish a school, Mr. Suydam. Isn't there a New Jersey law providing for free education of every child in the state?"

"A law, yes. It has never been enforced."

"Every law should be carried out to the letter, or annulled. How else can people have respect for the law? This particular law hasn't been repealed, I'm told. I intend to see that it is religiously enforced here in Bordentown."

"The sentiment does you credit, Miss Barton. A very laudable ambition." He shook his head. "You could not attain it alone and single-handed."

"I think I could, though it would be much less awkward if you helped me. I'm counting on that."

"I, Miss Barton?"

"In your official capacity." She paused. "Or would you prefer that I proceed without you?"

"Well," said Mr. Suydam, clearing his throat. "Well—"

"The thing is, for your own sake you'll not wish to withhold your co-operation, Mr. Suydam. Just suppose that you do refuse me? When I have my school all in shape, your Committee will be rather embarrassed not to have had a hand in it. The citizens of Bordentown will chalk a black mark against you. The newspapers will probably write editorials criticizing you. But if you get me a good building somewhere and desks and benches and books, then half the praise will be yours."

Astonishment consumed Mr. Suydam. Why, she spoke of

her school as if it were already in shape! "Miss Barton," he said, "the respectable people of this town would oppose you. Many of the mistresses of our private schools are ladies of much influence—they would be awfully displeased. As for your salary—"

"I don't want any salary."

"Tut-tut, Miss Barton!"

"No, honestly, I don't."

"Are you some sort of—of philanthropist?"

"Oh, no. Nor a martyr, either. Nothing heroic. But I know that Bordentown needs a public school, and that I can found one. I've done it before and I shall do it here, Mr. Suydam. Would you like to make it a wager? Let's say that if, after a fair trial, the Committee thinks I've succeeded, a salary will be paid me. But if the Committee thinks I haven't—if I haven't shown that free education of all the children has benefited the whole town, everybody, then I'll abolish my school, and nothing except my own time will have been squandered."

Mr. Suydam dabbed at his perspiring brow with a handkerchief from his waistcoat pocket. "You wish me to lay the er—*wager*—before the Committee, Miss Barton?"

"Yes, thank you. And right away?"

"Tomorrow." Mr. Suydam shrugged, noting how briskly the red feather tilted in the little lady's bonnet. Sweet and demure, you might have thought her, and devoid of guile. As she went out of his office, the postmaster's sigh echoed hollowly.

The very next afternoon she was again closeted with Mr. Suydam. This time the other Committee members were there. They were men of integrity, sworn to represent the citizenry of Bordentown. They had misgivings as to the "hazardous nature" of Miss Barton's proposal. Yet could they *legally* decline to sanction a public school?

"Let us vote." The chairman's tone was so doleful that he might have been saying, "Let us pray."

They voted. It was a unanimous vote. A schoolhouse would be prepared for Miss Barton. But to inveigle the wayward boys into it—that would be Miss Barton's problem. The Committee had discharged its duty.

Six pupils, and sixteen more, and then sixty, a hundred.

When the number was at two hundred, Clara wrote to Miss Fannie Childs, an Oxford friend. "Come, Fannie! I'm swamped!"

Miss Childs, an experienced teacher, arrived and took over half the pupils and taught them in a hall above a tailor shop. She and Clara roomed together in a house near by, and their winter was a bustling, merry one. They laughed a great deal. Other roomers in the house would hear the two schoolmarms giggling hilariously in the evenings, the clatter of their dishes as they cooked some impromptu, midnight meal.

Bordentown's first free school! Mr. Suydam was jubilant. "We must have more space," he said. For now the patrons did not consist entirely of "ruffians" and "renegades," the ragtag and bobtail that fringed respectability. Now the sons and daughters of affluent parents were deserting private academies for Clara's classes. When the new building was completed, it seated six hundred and was filled to overflowing and was the model for schools in other localities. Mr. Suydam said that Miss Barton must have a suitable remuneration, and accordingly she was voted a salary.

But in 1854, with the Bordentown school so flourishing that a superintendent must be appointed, the Committee looked over Clara Barton's head and chose elsewhere. The school was too large, the Committee said, for a woman to manage.

"Yes, it *is* large—because you made it so, Clara!" cried Fannie Childs, incensed. "And while it was in the process of growing large, you have managed it perfectly well. The Committee has discriminated against you simply because you're a woman. That's always the way! Women can do the hard labor, the spade work, and no one says a word. But when the honors are being handed out, some man steps in and takes all the glory. I despise the Committee!" Fannie stamped her foot. "How can they be so blind to your merits? I'll never forgive them!"

"Yes, you will, Fannie," Clara said. "And I will, too."

"But you'll remember how they've treated you."

"No, that's a thing I'll forget to remember. And the school will really be mine." Clara smiled. "Nothing can change that. Fannie, dear, I'm leaving Bordentown. For several months my voice has been troubling me. Some throat inflammation, the doctors tell me, and I ought to rest."

"You've worn yourself out for folks who don't appreciate you."

"They do appreciate me. The school will go on, and it will exemplify the sound American principles which I've believed in. Perhaps my ability, such as it is, is for *beginnings,* to get things organized and in running order, and then to relinquish the helm to someone else. I'm going to Oxford, to spend the summer with my father, and David and Stephen and their families. Later, I think I'll go to Washington."

"Washington?" Fannie repeated. "Whatever for?"

"Oh, to see the sights. I can afford it. You know, I've saved up quite a bit of money, Fannie, and I've made investments which bring me in dividends."

"Could you live on your income?"

"For a while, anyway. Maybe I'll cast about for something to do in Washington."

"I'm sure you will. You wouldn't be satisfied otherwise." Fannie paused, and said, "I've wondered why you don't marry. You've had your share of admirers."

Clara laughed gently. Yes, there had been admirers, and there would be more, for she had an appealing sort of dark and quiet beauty. She liked men, dozens of them were her friends. But her heart was untouched. The happiness of home and fireside and marriage was not for her. Not yet, and perhaps never. The path which she must tread seemed strange and solitary, but it was fixed, and she would not deviate from it.

9

WASHINGTON had more than forty thousand inhabitants when Clara Barton went there in 1854, but was still, as in Andrew Jackson's time, "a city of magnificent distances," its grandeur as yet only a promise. Georgetown was the best residential district. Most streets were unpaved, and even in the downtown areas tracts of forest trees stood fenced in behind unpainted palings. Few of the government buildings had been completed. The height of the Washington Monument was arrested in midflight and the top of the obelisk encased in wooden scaffolding. The Capitol had sprouted two unroofed wings, but still wore for a crown the little old dome, like a jug, where soon the mammoth rotunda would rise.

The Executive Mansion was coming to be known as the White House. In it, behind a straggling garden and a screen of Ionic pilasters which looked like stone but were an imitation, lived Franklin Pierce, the New Hampshire lawyer, who was President of the United States.

Sally Barton Vassall was then living with her husband and sons in Washington. It was to them that Clara went. But after she had got her bearings and decided to remain through the winter, she felt she could not impose further on her sister's hospitality, and she rented lodgings at 1013 T Street. She had no premonition of the many years in which this apartment,

74

one big room and three smaller ones, would be her home, or that henceforth for half a century this city would be the scene of her varied and almost ceaseless activity.

After a month or two of rest and leisure and sightseeing, Clara was looking for work, as Fannie Childs had predicted. Through the recommendation of her father's friend, Colonel Alexander De Witt, a Congressman from Massachusetts, she was named as copyist in the United States Patent Office.

There was even then great inventive genius in this comparatively new country. The Patent Office, which served that genius, was housed at the corner of Seventh and F Streets. "A stately marble palace," so Clara wrote to David, "with several suites of display salons, a library, and, in front, a courtyard of flowers and fountains."

The department had important functions in government, but Clara thought her own assignment rather drab. What was it, she asked David, except the interminable copying of letters into stupid old ledgers? ("... 3500 pages of dry lawyer writing is something to wade through in three months; and out of them I have filled a *great* volume almost as heavy as I can lift. My arm is tired, and my poor thumb is all calloused holding my pen.") But she was quickly made aware that other people considered her appointment sensational and somehow evil. She was the first woman ever to be a Patent Office clerk. As such, she was a pioneer—and an unwelcome one.

Going to her desk on her first morning there, she walked down a corridor lined with men who were determined to demonstrate their resentment of this interloper in a realm which had been solidly male. They were her fellow workers, but they didn't intend to be for long. They would rid themselves of the "pest in petticoats." They whistled at her, blew smoke in her face, spat tobacco juice at her feet—and were enraged when she seemed oblivious to these insults. Next morning the performance was repeated, and every morning. Clara was appalled and disgusted, but punctually each day she ran the gantlet in the corridor.

"I'm terrified," she confessed to David, "but I'll never let them know it." Nobody could be so stubborn as a Barton!

In six months she had been promoted and was the confidential clerk of Mr. Charles Mason, Superintendent of Patents. This was fuel to the flame of jealousy and prejudice. Now, indeed, the "pest" must be exterminated. Something drastic must be done. The men clerks conferred. Why not a whispering campaign?

"Miss Barton is incapable. . . . A meddler . . . A spy."

The fact was that her work, at which she was *most* capable, might have seemed rather like spying to a guilty conscience. There had been a leakage from the Patent Office. The trust of inventors had been betrayed through the stealing of diagrams and drawings, charts, and formulae of articles submitted for patenting. Mr. Mason was intent on stopping the thievery, and Clara must be his private investigator.

She did not especially relish the job, but she would not shirk it. Cheating she never could condone. And she surmised, truly enough, that much of her unpopularity was based on fear of what she might find out about the dishonesty of the other clerks. Quietly but steadily, she went her own way, obeying instructions, revealing unsavory conditions where they existed, sorry when her investigations led to someone's removal, yet knowing that it was her duty to stamp out fraud—and inexorably doing her duty. The whispering could not damage her, but it was a boomerang for some of her tormentors. Many of them were ousted. Clara stayed on.

In spite of the petty persecutions in the office, which never abated, Clara was happy to be in Washington. Her salary was $1,400 dollars a year, a great part of which she saved, with that economy so characteristic of her. She had all the necessities, and also those luxuries which she cared for—though the luxuries were few, her habits were frugal. Away from her desk, she was never lonely. She saw much of the Vassalls, and frequently Fannie Childs came from Oxford to Clara's apartment. Fannie's engagement to marry Bernard Vassall had recently been announced, and Clara was elated. It seemed to her an ideal match, for she adored Fannie and was fond of her nephew. She congratulated both of them. They had selected well, she said.

Besides these personal satisfactions, Clara was stimulated by the atmosphere of Washington. The city was dominated by politics, affairs of diplomacy and state, in which she always had been interested. Slavery was the engrossing topic of the day. Of course, it was everywhere, throughout the nation, the burning issue, never long forgotten. But in Washington, where the Congress met, the fire blazed highest.

Unlike many New Englanders, Clara Barton was not an Abolitionist. She abhorred salvery. It was a contradiction of all that she believed and had been taught, a scourge which should not be allowed to spread. Yet she did not think that the sudden emancipation of all the Negroes would straighten out the snarled hatreds which slavery had caused. Perhaps that would only make matters worse. Tolerance was the bedrock of her creed. She tried to see the question of slavery from the viewpoint of the South as well as that of the North, and she felt that violent agitators and impassioned orators were pushing the country toward the brink of division.

Lately her brother Stephen had purchased a steam mill in North Carolina. He had cultivated the property and then moved his family there. The prosperous little village growing up around the mill was known as Bartonville, and Stephen, a Yankee born and bred, was its leading citizen.

In a letter to him, Clara begged Stephen to be cool and wary of arguments which might involve him with his slave-owning neighbors. "It will be a strange pass," she said, "when the Bartons get fanatical and cannot abide by and support the laws they live under." Wouldn't Stephen pray, as she did, that a crisis which seemed imminent would somehow be averted?

There were at this time two major political parties in the United States: the Whigs and the Democrats. Clara's father had been an enthusiastic Democrat always, and so she had sympathized with that party's precepts. But now a third party was forming. In 1854, at Jackson, Michigan, a convention of men, among them dissenters from the American or Know-Nothing Party, organized what was to be the Republican Party. Probably Clara Barton heard little and thought less about this feeble Michigan political infant, yet her existence was to be affected by it.

Whenever she could, she liked to go to the gallery of the Senate chamber and listen to the debate on the floor. She was there on May 19, 1856, when Charles Sumner, Senator from Massachusetts, delivered his speech, "The Crime Against Kansas," denouncing those lawmakers who had voted for the carrying of slavery into the new state of Kansas, and thus, he alleged, set aside as void the Missouri Compromise.

That speech of Sumner's was received with varying emotions. Most Northerners applauded it. Not all: Stephen A. Douglas was so shocked by the harshness of the language that he inquired whether it was Senator Sumner's object "to provoke some of us to kick him as we would a dog in the street," and others felt that the orator had stirred up rancors which were better left to rest. The Southern statesmen and all the people whom they represented were wrathy, and two days later Preston Brooks, a member of the House, was still so furious that he struck Sumner down in the Senate chamber, raining blows upon his head until he was unconscious, an assault from which the Massachusetts man never wholly recovered.

But to one of his audience, at least, Sumner's speech seemed epochal. Clara Barton, sitting in the gallery, going home through silent, night-locked streets, knew that a dread crisis had drawn nearer. She wrote in her journal that war had begun that night.

"It began not at Sumter," she said later, "but at Sumner."

A few months afterward, James Buchanan was elected President. He was a Pennsylvanian, a Democrat, a man of education, but one inclined to vacillate, to be swayed by Southern politicians. He looked for an easy way to harmony—when there was none. With Buchanan's election, rumor buzzed in the Patent Office that any clerk who had favored the Republican presidential candidate would be dismissed. And Clara had frankly hoped that John C. Frémont would win.

A friend who wished to save her said that she must renounce her belief in Republicanism. "Why, you're an old Loco, Clara," he told her. "A dyed-in-the-wool Democrat, like your daddy. Anyway, a woman can't vote, she's bound to be what her menfolks are. Saying you're a Republican is just a fad with you."

"No," she replied, "I don't think it's a fad. But if so, I can't discard it now. I was for Frémont against Buchanan. I made the statement and meant it. I couldn't recant, either to keep my clerkship or for any other reason."

"Your obstinate little head will certainly be lopped off."

It certainly was. In 1857 Miss Clara Barton's resignation from the Patent Office was requested.

She went back to Oxford, to her father, to David and Julia and their children, and she said that it was good to be at home, she was glad. But as Buchanan's term approached its end, a letter came to her. Would she return to the Patent Office? The records there were all askew; an expert was needed to extricate the department from its predicament. Perhaps Miss Barton would let bygones be bygones—and oblige?

Her father said that she must go. And she wanted to. She loved Oxford, would always love it. But Washington was the most fascinating place in the universe.

So she was again in her pleasant rooms in T Street, watching the nation's pitiful advance toward the "irrepressible conflict," feeling the ever-tightening tension.

In October 1859, John Brown of Kansas, the half-mad Abolitionist, envisaged the overthrow of a government which did not suit him and led his foray against Harpers Ferry, Virginia, and the Federal arsenal there. In December he was hanged for treason. Though his body lay a-mouldering in the grave, his soul went marching on, and unnumbered thousands charged his death to slavery and pledged to avenge it.

Congressmen in the closing months of that year and the spring of 1860 wore daggers and pistols in belts beneath their frock coats. Disputes hinged upon slavery, and almost everyone brought out the antagonism between the North and the South.

In November 1860, four candidates ran for the Presidency, and Abraham Lincoln polled the majority of electoral votes. No man could have been less acceptable to the South. The *Charleston Courier* had printed its warning in a broadside: *"If Lincoln Is Elected South Carolina Will Lead Boldly for a Southern Confederacy."* It was no idle threat. On December 20, South Carolina seceded from the Union and dispatched delegates to Washington to claim possession of Fort Sumter in

Charleston harbor and all other United States property in the state. "The Union," screamed the South Carolina newspapers, "is dissolved!" Buchanan denied the right of secession (though weakly) and he sent reinforcement to Fort Sumter. The supply ship was fired on and turned back at the harbor's mouth.

Six more states seceded. Their delegates meeting with those of South Carolina organized the Confederate States of America. Jefferson Davis, the Confederacy's President, was inaugurated on February 18, 1861.

Buchanan was anxious, but he did little to relieve the nation's stress. His wish was to be away from it all, to leave positive action to his successor.

On March 4, 1861—a day after the Southern general Beauregard had finished his plans for an attack on Fort Sumter—Abraham Lincoln became President of the United States.

Clara Barton wrote home to Oxford, "The 4th of March has come and gone, and we have a *live Republican* President. We had a crowd, of course, but not so utterly overwhelming as had been anticipated; everywhere seemed to be just full, and no more. . . . The ceremony was performed upon the East Capitol steps facing Capitol Hill. . . . The inaugural address was delivered in a loud, fine voice, which was audible to many of the assemblage. Only a very few of the United States troops were brought to the Capitol at all, but were in readiness at their quarters and other parts of the city; they were probably not brought out, lest it look like menace. Great pains appeared to be taken to avoid all such appearances, and indeed a more orderly crowd I think I never saw and general satisfaction expressed at the trend and spirit of the Address."

Mr. Lincoln's inauguration. . . .

The military escort had come to fetch him from his hotel, with Mr. Buchanan stepping from the state carriage, where the liveried coachmen sat on the box. Mr. Buchanan went in person to Mr. Lincoln's room, rapped on his door. As they stepped into the carriage again, the band played *Hail, Columbia,* and mounted soldiers swooped into rank behind them. There were other outriders, too, gentlemen in top hats, and broad colorful sashes, astride prancing black horses. It was a warm day, weather like summertime, dust underfoot, as the procession wound along Pennsylvania Avenue through the massed curbs. Mr. Lincoln bowed continuously.

The Diplomatic Corps and the Justices of the Supreme Court, headed by Chief Justice Roger Taney, were congregated in the Senate chamber, where, at ten minutes past one, Mr. Buchanan and Mr. Lincoln were ushered in. Without pause, the dignitaries filed onto the platform, and Senator Baker introduced the President-elect to the multitude.

He stood motionless an instant, this gaunt and bearded rail splitter, this Honest Abe. Then he handed his brand-new silk hat and his huge gold-topped cane to Stephen A. Douglas, one of the three adversaries he had defeated at the polls, who now, dapper and smiling, stood beside him. Mr. Lincoln fumbled in his pocket for his spectacles, clamped them on his big nose. He produced his manuscript and, in that "loud, fine voice," he read.

He would not, he said, interfere with the domestic institutions of the South, or with any of the safeguards of the Constitution, but he believed in the Union. By his reasoning, a state could not possibly secede from the Union, which had been created to endure forever. An attempt at such desertion must, therefore, be viewed as insurrection or, if on a large scale, revolution.

His purpose as President would be to see that the laws of the Union were faithfully executed in all the states. To the

South, he said, "In your hands, my dissatisfied fellow country-men, and not in mine, is the momentous issue of civil war. The Government will not assail you. You can have no conflict without being yourselves the aggressors."

To North and South, he said, "We are not enemies, but friends. We must not be enemies. Though passion may have strained, it must not break our bonds of affection. The mystic chords of memory, stretching from every battlefield and patriotic grave, to every living heart and hearthstone all over this broad land, will yet swell the chorus of the Union, when again touched, as surely they will be, by the better angels of our nature."

Then Chief Justice Taney, picturesque in his black robes, administered the oath of office, with Mr. Lincoln's palm big and very firm upon the Bible. And the procession made its formal pilgrimage along Pennsylvania Avenue again, this time toward the White House, where Mr. Buchanan bade the new President a courteous and unregretful Godspeed.

So the day came and went, March 4, 1861. Abraham Lincoln was President of the United States. And the stage was set for tremendous and terrible events.

10

On April 12, 1861, the strained relations between the North and the South were at the breaking point.

Perhaps of all Americans, Major Robert Anderson was surest of the climax, for he was commanding the beleaguered Federal garrison in Fort Sumter. Without food and ammunition he was stranded in a little fastness claimed by the North—and knew that he could not hold out against General Beauregard's batteries of Confederate cannon.

Major Anderson, a patriot, would not surrender until he had to. But when fire belched forth at him before dawn on that fateful morning, he estimated his resistance as only a matter of hours. Through Saturday and Sunday he hesitated, while Sumter's walls crumbled and smoke enshrouded the portholes and powder magazines exploded and his men faced a senseless death of starvation. Then reluctantly Major Anderson reefed in the Stars and Stripes, and a square of white slowly ascended the flagpole.

Fort Sumter had bowed to Beauregard, and the War Between the States was a fact.

The South was the aggressor, as Abraham Lincoln had said it must be, but the effort of the North would be to invade the seceding states and recapture that territory and those possessions which the Confederacy had appropriated. The Union had an army of thirteen thousand troops, most of them in scattered outposts on the Indian frontiers. President Lincoln must ask for seventy-five thousand volunteers. The telegraph wires had scarcely ticked before regiments from every Northern and Middle Western state were on their way to the Capital. Four of these regiments, all from Massachusetts, were mobbed by civilians at Baltimore on April 19; three of the militiamen were killed and thirty more injured.

Clara was at the station when the train steamed in from Baltimore. She was in a mood of excitement. She believed, as did everyone in the city, that Washington might be attacked at any moment. Knowing nothing of war, she said, "If it must be, let it come."

A cheer went up as the soldiers, tired and hot in their heavy flannel clothing, poured from the coaches, and Clara's breath lumped in her throat—for one regiment was composed of Worcester County men. A lanky lad in the ranks cried at her, his voice penetrating the din:

"Hi, Miss Barton!"

Young Simon from the farm adjoining David's! When had she seen him last? At a church picnic.

The victims of the Maryland mob were lowered on stretchers to the platform and taken to an infirmary. Their comrades filed up the street toward the Capitol grounds, where they would be encamped until further orders disposed of them. The crowd of onlookers followed.

As the lawn around the building filled, space was sought inside. Like the seepage of water, the uniformed squads trickled into the halls, into every available area. Guns were stacked in corners and the men flung themselves down on the floor. Conversation hummed and was punctuated by good-humored laughter. Somebody sang, a popular paraphrase to the tune of *The Star-Spangled Banner:*

"O say, have you heard how the Flag of our sires
    Was insulted by traitors, in boastful alliance,
    When for Union's dear cause, over Sumter's red fires,
    In the front of Rebellion it waved its defiance . . ."

Townsfolk peeped in from the portal or sidled along the walls, fluttering women, children who would glimpse these heroes—the first to respond to their country's call, the first to shed blood in its defense. The war was so new. Nobody thought it would last long. But while it lasted, it would be thrilling.

Clara was at the door of the Senate chamber. Young Simon had gone in there. She wanted to show him the paper clutched in her gloved fingers and to tell him that tomorrow she would bring him something to eat, a little treat of jelly or preserved peaches. She remembered that Simon had a sweet tooth.

A voice behind her exclaimed, "Your being here makes me think o' home, Miss Barton."

It was the lad himself. "Oh, I was hunting for you," Clara said. "I've a copy of the *Worcester Spy* with the account in it of what happened to the regiment in Baltimore."

"Well! . . . Hi!" he yelled, as a dozen other hands snatched at the paper. "You'll tear it. We can't all read it at the same time. I've got an idea." Grasping Clara's wrist, he piloted her down the aisle to the big central desk, the one belonging to the presiding officer of the Senate. Turning, he swung her up to the desk top. "There you are—and light as a feather! Fellows! Miss Barton's going to read us a story."

The vast balconied room was quickly hushed. All eyes focused on the slender little figure on her lofty perch. She blushed and began to read.

Never had she had a more rapt audience. They were like

children, a class of schoolboys. She had to repeat the story—it was about themselves. Their home-town newspaper. When she finished the second reading, they thanked her with a burst of hand clapping.

She knew so many of them. They had been her pupils, the sons of her neighbors, husbands or brothers of old schoolmates. She told them she was proud of them.

"I want to get you something. What do you need?"

"Towels," Simon said. "Nary a towel did we bring with us."

"Soap," said someone else. "And handkerchiefs. Me with a cold in my nose—and no kerchief!"

"Scissors," said a soldier in sergeant's chevrons. "Needles and thread and buttons. We left in a hurry and didn't think of such items. And blankets—"

"Golly!" roared Simon. "We mustn't make pigs of ourselves. Miss Barton ain't the quartermaster corps!"

She was not the quartermaster corps. But, hastening home, she rummaged and stripped the shelves of her linen closet. She slashed sheets into pieces the size of towels and handkerchiefs. She went out to market and bought quantities of food.

Next morning (it was Sunday) an odd little parade breasted the tide of churchgoers in downtown Washington. Clara was leading it, her arms piled high with parcels. Behind her were five Negro porters lugging immense hampers. The Senate chamber was her destination. And she did not mind in the least if anyone charged her with desecrating the Sabbath.

The Massachusetts militia moved farther south, into Virginia. But they were replaced by other regiments, for the Union army was woefully short of tents and barracks. Grass plots about the government buildings must suffice as campsites for the troops constantly passing through the city. Clara was as concerned for the newcomers as she had been for her Oxford men. Each day she went to them, laden with supplies. When her own cupboards were depleted and she had no more cash for purchases, she hit upon the thought of advertising in the *Worcester Spy:* gifts intended for the soldiers could be sent to her address, where she personally would supervise their distribution. Soon letters were flowing in to her from scores of New England mothers, wives, and sisters. Crates and boxes were carted to her doorstep—until she had to rent a storeroom to hold them.

There was nothing official about this undertaking, no motive for it except her disinterested wish that soldiers, if they must go to war, should go as well equipped as was possible.

The city and everyone in it was swept by a fever of patriotism. No one doubted now that the war had been inevitable, that it was justified, and that its outcome would be swift victory for the North. Daily there were incidents to fan the emotions. One of these was the funeral of Colonel Elmer Ellsworth.

He had been a young officer of Zouaves stationed at Alexandria. Climbing the stairs of the hotel to get the Confederate flag which still flew there, Ellsworth was shot down. When his body was borne along Pennsylvania Avenue, to the beat of muffled drums, the bier guarded by furled banners, the riderless horse stalking after, thousands of people stood in silence, and a nation mourned him.

"Surely," wrote Clara to David, "it was great love and respect to be meted out to the memory of one so young."

Weeks elapsed with no military skirmishes of any import. A chief objective of the North would be Richmond, the capital of the Confederacy. The army pushed tentatively southward. Then on July 21, at Bull Run a battle was fought.

It was a rout for the North. Clara in Washington viewed its consequences, the flight back to the Potomac of those very regiments which had marched so confidently away. Not all returned: five hundred men had been killed, fifteen hundred were missing. A thousand wounded were rushed to Washington hospitals.

Clara offered her services as a nurse in any of the hospitals, but they had more applicants than could be used. She occupied herself with the distributing agency she had established: it was growing to astonishing proportions and had become a clearing-house widely advertised in countless villages and hamlets. But she had occasion to visit some of the wounded—her "own boys." From them she learned of the suffering they had endured before they were conveyed to the hospitals.

This was awful. And, she wondered, *couldn't it be avoided?* She would investigate.

Clara had retained her Patent Office connection. Months ago she had asked to do the work of two clerks and turn back both pay checks to the government. ("What," she demanded, "is money if you have no country?") But such a scheme was unusual, impractical, and—said the head of the department—might be illegal. Now, however, she was glad for her clerkship. Through it she could approach several men of influence.

During the summer she talked with these influential acquaintances, one by one. Her query was simple enough: Why couldn't the wounded have immediate care? "There are at present in the Georgetown hospital seven men," she said, "former pupils of mine, each of whom has lost an arm or a leg and is permanently crippled. First aid behind the lines at Bull Run could have averted the amputations. By what measures will similar misfortunes be prevented?" The replies she gleaned were not encouraging.

On a November afternoon she sat across the table from an army surgeon who was her friend. The Union cause had not been faring well. At Ball's Bluff four Federal regiments had ferried over the Potomac, only to be beaten back, into the river where more than half were drowned. The North, shorn of its optimism, was realizing that it was in for a long and grim struggle.

"Willie Grout was one who drowned," Clara said. "I remember the day Willie came to my school. A mischievous, fun-loving boy. But he is dead now—mercifully. It's the men still living I'm thinking of."

Her friend nodded. "We have the United States Sanitary Commission and the Christian Commission, Miss Barton. They also are thinking of the living, wanting to save them."

"What are these commissions, exactly? What are they doing?"

"Well, the first, the Sanitary Commission, is a group of civilians who act in an advisory capacity to the Surgeon General's department. The group will educate public opinion on matters pertaining to the army and arouse the government to take necessary steps toward correcting adverse conditions in the camps. Here, in brief, is their intent." Clara's friend read from a leaflet, " 'The one point which controls the commission is just this: A simple desire and resolute determination to secure for the men who have enlisted in this war that care which it is the duty of the nation to give them. That care is their right, and in the government or out of it, it must be given them, let who will stand in the way.' "

"I like the sound of that," Clara said. "And what headway has been made?"

"The commission is not looked on with too much favor as yet, for it has no actual authority," the surgeon said. "But I think it will do splendid things as it goes on. Already it has conducted surveys and offered suggestions, such as that part of the soldier's pay be remitted to his family, that the camps establish proper regulations and adequate policing, that proper bathing facilities be provided, and that the mess be ample and wholesome, the diet balanced. These are only a few of the Sanitary Commission's recommendations—it remains to be seen whether they will be adopted. But it is my own belief that we shall notice an improvement in the health, morale, and contentment of the men, due to the Commission's efforts."

"And the Christian Commission?" Clara asked.

"It was organized by the Young Men's Christian Association, and its aims are rather like those of the Sanitary Commission, with the added purpose of promoting the spiritual and moral welfare of the soldiers. Its members are clergymen, who see to the building of chapels where church services can be held and try to institute in the camps some system of innocent recreation and sports which will be of benefit."

"Each of the movements is worthy and will succeed, I hope," Clara said, "but neither is quite what I had in mind. Something else should and must be done—and very soon, too. Nursing—"

"The army has excellent nurses, Miss Barton. Dorothea Dix is superintendent of our staff."

"I know Miss Dix."

"A famous American."

"And a remarkable woman," Clara said. "Miss Dix lived for a while in Worcester. In fact, it was there that she began her reforms of jails and almshouses and insane asylums. She is a sort of genius, capable at anything she attempts. Her name will go down in history. But not Miss Dix, not anybody, has got at the root of the difficulty. Don't you see what I mean?"

She leaned an elbow on the table, her dark eyes intense. "A man is shot or bayoneted. Critically wounded, he falls. For hours, maybe for a day, two days, he lies where he has fallen—"

"He will be found and picked up by the stretcher bearers."

"Yes. But often the waiting to be found is the difference between recovery and death. I've gone down to the docks, when the transports arrived with the wounded. Some have been neglected too long. Hundreds die before they can be taken to the hospital's excellent nursing. I cannot reconcile myself to those deaths, that neglect, that delay."

"It's true," the surgeon agreed. "But there's no organization for relief directly a soldier falls, Miss Barton."

"One could be formed. That isn't hard to do. In my own small way, I've proved how easily an organization comes into being. People are so eager to help. All they lack is guidance as to the best method of helping. Right now, throughout New England, women are meeting together in fifty schoolhouses or churches to knit and sew, to pack cartons of canned foodstuffs and bread and crackers and coffee, and nail the cartons shut and ship them to me. I have these stores and the funds to buy more. Tell me, why can't they be distributed at the place where they would be of most value?"

"And that is—"

"In the field!"

"There would be no one to handle them."

"Let me go!"

"Behind the lines? Alone?"

"Alone, if I must. But grant me permission and let me go!"

"Miss Barton, you don't know what you're saying. A woman on the battlefield? Are you utterly fearless, then?"

"I've always been utterly cowardly. But I think I could be brave if I felt that by doing so I was stopping this cruel waste."

"You might *try*—"

"And not finish the job? No. I scorn people who get hold of a log they can't lift and then set up a wail for someone to lift it for them. I shouldn't do that."

"I'm sorry, Miss Barton." Her friend shrugged. "It is not in my province either to grant or withhold permission. But I'm rather sure you'll never get it, anywhere."

She went sadly out into the autumn afternoon. The breeze was bland; the bluish haze of Indian summer sifted the sun's slanting rays. Streets were swollen with traffic, for Washington had nearly doubled its population in the months since the declaration of war. Old mansions were being dismantled and converted into apartments; new tiers of flats were mushrooms in every vacant lot. Outside the city, in valleys and on hills, were other cities, of peaked canvas, the thousands of tents sheltering troops. From a distance they looked like herds of cattle, the white tents against rust-green verdure.

As Clara strolled down the Mall, she heard the blare of martial music, a band playing:

> "We'll rally 'round the flag, boys,
> We'll rally once again,
> Shouting the battle cry of freedom."

The air and the words of the song bespoke the spirit of the times. And that night Clara wrote in her journal, "We cannot desert our great, poor charge of humanity, but must stay and suffer with them, if need be."

11

CLARA BARTON would have been less harrowed by the war if she could have thought of it merely as the maneuvering of masses of nameless men. Instead, she thought of the individual soldier, what he did and saw and felt, beneath "the leaden rain and iron hail," and it seemed to her incredible that any effort should be spared which might lighten his lot. During the winter more and more supplies came to her. She took them to the hospitals and the camps in Washington—and thought it foolish that she should be so constricted. Still she saw the dying whom the transports brought to the Potomac docks, and she thought bitterly that with prompt attention these might have lived.

She was at her Patent Office desk every day, with only the early mornings and late afternoons and Sundays for her excursions to the troops. Evenings she spent unpacking and sorting the contents of the boxes which were sent her, and often she was busy at this until after midnight. She said it was a lucky thing she never had required much sleep.

She was in her storeroom one stormy February night when a tapping sounded on the door. The man standing there was a stranger to her. He was young and blond, awkward in what was obviously a new uniform.

"Miss Barton? You don't know me."

"No, I don't."

"I'm from Indiana. My name's Farley. Maybe you remember George Ferguson? He was in your school."

"At Bordentown. I do indeed remember him."

"George is out in my state now. A town called Brazil. He and I are good friends. He told me about you, and how many people you're helping all the time, and that probably you'd do something for me."

Clara smiled. "I will if I can, Mr. Farley."

From his blouse he took an envelope and a small sealed packet. "In this envelope is my warrant as a noncom officer." He placed it on the counter which ran along under the shelves. "I'm mighty puffed up about being a sergeant. Well, I want you to keep the warrant and the little packet for me, until I get back to Washington. But if you read my name in the Black List, will you send them to someone I love in Indiana?"

"Your mother, perhaps?"

"No, I'm an orphan. No relatives at all. But there's a girl—"

"Ah," said Clara. So often there was a girl.

"We're going to be married after the war. That is—" He paused.

"I understand. Just write the address on a slip of paper. I'll do exactly what you say. And I shall pray that you'll soon return to carry home these belongings yourself."

"Thank you, Miss Barton. I know I can trust you." Sergeant Farley made the notation and handed her the slip. He glanced around him. "Like a shop, isn't it?"

"Yes, I have a little bit of everything here—from neck comforters to boot laces, from thimbles to wax tapers. Medicines, too."

"They say you wanted to go to the front."

"I've moved heaven and earth! But the authorities are against it. There are two objections. The first, that nobody has done it before, seems ridiculous, because every experiment must start sometime, somewhere. And the second objection I have even less patience witn—that I'm a woman, that the conventions and proprieties mustn't be flouted."

"It *is* silly," he agreed. "So you've given up the notion, eh?"

"Oh, no! I continue to hope. I'm a mulish creature."

"You look anything but that." He shook his head. "Good-by, Miss Barton. My regiment has been ordered to Annapolis. We're sailing before the end of the week for Roanoke."

"Roanoke! How I wish I were going with you."

"Why?" He was at the door, but the eagerness of her tone deterred him.

"My brother Stephen is down there in that vicinity. We have heard nothing from him for months, and his last communication was rather frightening. I was thinking about Stephen this evening, just before you came in. I think about him a great deal."

"Tell me why you're frightened for your brother, Miss Barton."

The gentleness in the young man's voice, his sensitive smile, made Clara feel that they were not strangers at all. Somehow, in a few minutes she found herself seated beside him, with two cups of tea she had brewed and a tin of crackers on the counter between them. And she was talking more freely than was her habit, telling him about Stephen.

She was not sure even that he was alive. "I know he'd been ailing. You see, he has this land and a mill in Hertford County, North Carolina. He's a businessman; he has made money. Of course, his sentiments are antislavery, and when the war broke he denounced secession. His Southern neighbors were angered —naturally, I think—and told him to get out. But Stephen wouldn't. He said he was an American citizen with the right to own property in any section of the country that pleased him, and that in his opinion North Carolina was still a part of the Union, and always would be. So then, since they couldn't rid themselves of him, they hemmed him in. They confiscated his mill and his horses and cattle and cut off his mail. That much we know. But nothing else. A month ago I sent him a message, by way of a Massachusetts officer who was going south. I asked him to set out, on foot if he had to, for Roanoke where Union troops might concentrate. But I've had no reply. Perhaps he never got the message. Stephen's danger is that the Southerners regard him as an enemy—while any Northerners who had no definite information about him would be suspicious of his loyalty." Clara sighed. "He is a middle-aged man now, not well, very headstrong—and very dear to me!"

Sergeant Farley had been listening sympathetically. "Turnabout is fair play, Miss Barton. You're doing a favor for me. Why not let me carry a second message? I can't promise to locate your brother, but I could try."

"Oh, would you?"

"Certainly. And if something happens to me—"

"No, sergeant. You're coming back—to the girl in Indiana."

"By Jove, when you say that I believe it. And believing's half of doing, isn't it?"

"More than half. It's everything."

She wrote the letter, cautiously, for there must be nothing in it which could bring trouble to the bearer. She suggested to Stephen the location of the Massachusetts regiments. If he could reach them, he would be among friends.

"*Come home;* I want you in Washington . . . I could cover pages telling you all the anxiety felt for you, all the hours of solicitude that I have known in the last ten months, wondering where you were, or if you were at all." She mentioned their father's failing health. "He has talked a *hundred volumes* about you, Stephen, wishes he could see you, knows he cannot, but hopes. . . ."

She folded the letter, and Sergeant Farley put it in his pocket. "I've got a four-leaf clover in there," he said, "and a rabbit's foot. I'm not superstitious, but I'm not overlooking any charms or talismans." He laughed, and, at the door, he shook her hand and raised it to his lips. "Thank you, again. You're all right, Miss Barton. You really are."

Then he went out into the sleety winter darkness.

Clara put into a wall safe Farley's envelope and packet. Many such treasures were there, mementos left with her. The owners might, or might not, reclaim them.

It was late, yet she felt wide awake. She picked up a magazine from the counter and leafed through it. It was a copy of the *Atlantic Monthly*. Some verses caught her eye: *The Battle Hymn of the Republic*. Clara knew the poem and the circumstances in which it had been composed: How Julia Ward Howe, a minor poet, had driven out one day with some Boston friends to witness a review of soldiers. As the carriage rolled between the stalwart files, Mrs. Howe, statuesque and beautiful, elegant as a picture in *Godey's Lady's Book*, had begun suddenly to sing:

"'John Brown's body lies a-mouldering in the grave . . .'"
A stirring melody, said Mrs. Howe to her wealthy friends; it should have nobler words. And that night, miraculously, she had roused from slumber with the noble words pounding in her brain. An inspiration from some divine source—there seemed no other explanation. "I scrawled the verses almost without looking at the paper," Mrs. Howe asserted. "Having

completed my writing, I fell asleep, saying to myself, 'I like this better than almost anything else that I have written.'"

Clara liked it too. But in this *Atlantic Monthly* was a couplet which touched her even more deeply; James Russell Lowell's homely meditation:

> "Old Uncle S,—says he, I guess,
> God's price is high, says he."

Before spring, her father's illness summoned Clara to Oxford. His joy in greeting her was pathetic. He had loved all his children and his grandchildren—but this was Clara, his baby girl, whose birth he had celebrated with the new Willow china, in whom he had a special pride.

She realized that he was declining, they must make the most of what time was vouchsafed them together. And so she sat beside him, stroking his pillow, while with a voice still resonant he explored the past. It was so vivid to him! His youth when he had campaigned with Anthony Wayne, when he had courted and won pretty Sarah Stone, and reared his sons and daughters. He spoke of Clara's childhood. How blest that period in a world at peace. "Do you remember the Thanksgiving afternoon your horse bolted on the Webster road? You were just a tyke; two other little girls were with you, cantering through a blinding snow. Panic struck the horses. But you soon asserted yourself and got the bridles of all three —and led 'em in the gate, meek as molasses. And the day I registered you at boarding school? I supposed you'd cry. Why, I was nearer tears than you were! Do you remember?"

He had arranged his earthly affairs with precision and made his will. They propped him up in bed to sign his documents.

"This is the last day I shall ever do any business," he said. "My work is done."

He spoke of the war and of his country's future. And often of Stephen. "You must look after him, Clara."

"I will, Father."

"He wouldn't be dictated to by those rebels. I can't blame him for that. Stephen's a Barton. But now he's in a peck of trouble, and you must fish him out of it."

"Yes, I will."

She discussed with him her desire to go to the battlefields, and how the twistings of red tape had trapped and netted her at every step. He said that people were absurd to thwart her just because she was a woman. And as for the soldiers— "They'll never harm you. I know soldiers. They will respect you and your errand."

He thought she might as well stay on at the Patent Office. "Then if the chance to do the other thing bobs up, grab it! Say, maybe Governor Andrew could pull some strings for you."

On a day when Mr. Barton seemed stronger, Clara went to Boston to talk with John A. Andrew, Massachusetts' eminent war governor. And that night, sitting with her father, she told him that Governor Andrew had been most cordial. "He dashed off a letter to the Surgeon General, asking that I have a pass into Virginia."

"Good!" said Mr. Barton. "Now we'll get somewhere."

She assented. "Yes, I think we will."

As the month closed, the old man was noticeably feebler, but calm and never complaining. Then, one evening, he called Clara and Julia to him and gave a hand to each. Sitting up in bed, he smiled and shut his eyes.

It was just such a leave-taking, Clara thought, as he would have chosen, so quiet and so dignified.

The burial was in the North Oxford churchyard. Clara went from the grave to David's house. A letter was there for her. It was from Governor Andrew. She opened it with trembling fingers.

The Surgeon General had thought about the Governor's petition. But, "I do not think that at the present time Miss Barton had better undertake to go to Burnside's Division to act as a nurse."

How terse that sentence!

Yet those bedside conferences with her father had infused her with a resolution which would not be blighted. And three months after the Surgeon General's rejection, the red tape had somehow been snipped and she had obtained the permission which she coveted. She never divulged just how it came about —and perhaps she herself never knew.

12

IT WAS characteristic of her that, having the passes which would take her wherever she wanted to go, Clara did not scurry off erratically, but made plans. This would not be a wild-goose chase—or a log she would strive to lift, only to wail for other lifters.

First, she hired a substitute to do her work at the Patent Office, and she got a leave of absence from the department. Then she went to Bordentown, to New York, Boston, Worcester, to all those towns and cities which were supplying her storeroom. She must be sure that she was to have reserves. She didn't picture herself as a militant angel of superhuman powers. She knew that whether or not she accomplished anything would depend largely upon the very human powers of hundreds of other women. As they were strong, so she would be.

Her first trip down into war-raddled Virginia occurred on Sunday, August 3, 1862. She had rented a wagon, a team of mules, and had employed a driver. Holding her skirts in a gloved hand, she hoisted herself over the wheel.

"Very well," she said.

The driver cried, "Giddap!" The mules trotted, and the wagon joggled over the cobbles toward the Potomac.

Julia Barton had said to Clara, "When you finally start, you'll probably feel like weeping." But she didn't. She felt sober and on her mettle.

She stopped overnight at Acquia Creek, where the quartermaster was courteous to her. Then she journeyed on to Fredericksburg.

By Tuesday night she was back in Washington. Her scrutiny of the Fredericksburg hospital had been enlightening. Medicines were needed there, and food suitable to invalids. She had nothing but reverence for the doctors and the orderlies toiling in the wards, but innumerable regulations tied the hands of these people, for in such vexing times the government was according more thought to hale men who could fight than to the disabled.

Clara Barton would be a free-lance, not subject to the limitations of the military, and this would be her advantage.

She conferred with the United States Sanitary Commissioners in Washington. Probably her path would often cross theirs; she wished to be on amiable terms with them. The Commissioners were broadening the scope of their work for the soldiers. Clara told them that she was not in any sense a rival; she wanted only to co-operate. She said she would not be constantly with the army, but would go to the battlefield as there were emergencies. Perhaps her prime problem would be to get transportation.

The fortunes of war had been running against the Union. General McClellan's thrust through the Virginia peninsula for Richmond was over—dismally, for the North. Robert E. Lee and Stonewall Jackson were exhibiting their strategy by taking the offensive and facing toward Washington. The summer had dealt a series of reverses to Northern aspirations. On August 9, Jackson again defeated the Union forces at Cedar Mountain, near the town of Culpeper.

Clara Barton had the news of the battle on Monday, August 11: the wounded and the missing totaled more than two thousand. This, she decided, was the hour for "breaking the shackles" and going to the front. She noted the decision in her journal, "Concluded to go to Culpeper. Packed goods."

Five days of incessant labor ensued; five sleepless nights in the field. The men who still had breath in their bodies must be got back, somehow, to hospital cots. Clara ministered to the Confederate wounded as well as to the Union, for she had no inclination to slight the one and soothe the other. All were suffering, and therefore all were alike in her eyes. It seemed to her that the pitiful debris could never be cleared away! And when a captain of cavalry said to her, "Miss Barton, this is a rough and unseemly position for you, a woman, to occupy," she could only reply with the sorrowful question, "Is it not as rough and unseemly for these pain-racked men?"

Cedar Mountain was but a foreshadowing. Before the month was out, Stonewall Jackson had attacked at Bull Run.

Clara went by train, in a baggage car with her crates, boxes and barrels—and a companion. As she climbed aboard and peered about the car's interior, a tall, spare figure clothed in rusty black rose from the corner dimness.

"Are you Clara Barton? Well, I'm Almira Fales." The woman shifted, a bar of mote-specked sunlight fell across her countenance, seamed and black-browed under a man's felt hat. "I heard you were off for the fighting. I'd like to go with you."

"I'd like to have you," Clara said.

"It won't be the first time I've gone." The woman seated herself on a keg. "I've been doing what I could—which wasn't much, for I had no passes through the pickets and no amount of stuff, as you have. Nor any money, either. My husband's in a government bureau in Washington and my sons have enlisted. But as long ago as December of 1860, just after Lincoln's election, I knew this war was coming. I commenced scraping lint and rolling bandages, and collecting magazines and books that I could give to convalescents in the infirmaries. Before there were convalescents, mind you! Before a shell had exploded! A lot of folks were amused, and the minister of my church laughed and said, 'Get your lint ready, if it will comfort your poor, worrying heart, though I don't believe it will ever be needed.' Just the same, I scraped lint. Now it's all used up."

The engine whistled and the car lurched. Clara sat down cross-legged on the floor among her stores.

"You're spry," Mrs. Fales remarked. "And young enough to be my daughter. You look like a smart, trig little school-ma'am."

"Perhaps I was that, once."

"But you've changed?" Mrs. Fales nodded. "Everybody has changed from what they were in the old days. The war does that. War is monstrous."

"This one had to happen."

"Oh, I suppose so—if any war has to." Mrs. Fales swayed, the brim of her odd hat vibrating with the motion of the clattering wheels. "Men could settle their differences peaceably, if they only would. But not all men want peace—more shame to them!"

Clara mused. Was not this what she had thought? That men have worshiped war until it has cost a million times more than the whole world is worth, and spilled the best blood, and crushed beneath miry heels the fairest ideals?

"Your dress is too nice," Mrs. Fales said critically, out of the silence. "Bull Run won't be a party, you know."

"I know. I have big gingham aprons in my bag."

"Why do you wear that red bow in your collar?"

"I'm fond of red." Clara smiled. "I think my father would have been glad for me to wear the ribbon today."

"I prefer plain things."

Clara was interested. Maybe Mrs. Fales would tell more about herself. But as the train bowled on, through the brassy heat of sun-baked meadows, through wood and ravines, over rickety, jerry-built bridges above rocky streams, the older woman had little to say. Dark and taciturn, something mysterious in her manner, she crouched in her corner.

Clara was to count Mrs. Fales as friend and ally in the months ahead, yet never to fathom her strangeness or her appearances and disappearances, which were equally abrupt and unheralded.

At ten o'clock of a Sunday morning, the train stopped at Fairfax station. Clara's car was shunted to a siding, the other cars kept to the main track, where they would be loaded for the return trip.

"They'll have a load, too," said Mrs. Fales.

"Yes," said Clara.

She stood gazing up the slope of a wide, thinly wooded hill. There, row upon row, laid out by the terrifying thousand, were inert, blue-uniformed forms, the wounded bedded on hay, like littered, sick cattle. Arching over the crest of the hill, from several directions, were strings of wagons, each one creaking with its gruesome weight. In the sky a great sable-winged bird soared and circled.

A man in soiled white clothing came down the slope. He was a member of the Sanitary Commission.

"Miss Barton, these are the soldiers who must be sent back as soon as possible." He was sweating and weary. "There are others—" He sighed. "As is so often the case, we have not enough drugs or cotton or gauze."

"I have several packages," Clara said. "Mrs. Fales and I will unpack them and get to work."

All day the two women worked, cleansing and dressing, applying oils and salves and disinfectants, taping up shattered bones, stanching blood. As fast as a sufferer was bandaged, he was carried on a stretcher to a flatcar. The Sanitary Commissioner, his orderlies, even the train crew, aided. Yet the rows seemed to grow ever longer, for the wagons came on relentlessly, without interruption, and every one was crowded. Presently the train rumbled away; it could not have accommodated another passenger. And night crept over the valley, a chill mist billowed up, an eerie wind soughed through the treetops.

By the light of a candle, Clara penciled a list, an inventory. They would be here in this spot, she and Mrs. Fales and the handful of able-bodied men, marooned as if on some remote planet, to guard the wounded—and to feed them. Well, she had pounds of preserves in the baggage car, gallons of fruit juices, cans of soup and beef, crackers and wine. And as vessels in which to serve this food, she had two water buckets, five tin cups, one iron kettle, and three shallow plates! Why hadn't she thought about such a contingency and provided for it?

"But it's futile," she murmured, "to reproach myself for that now. The men must be fed. Some of them have had no nourishment for forty-eight hours, and all are sinking because of the exposure."

She kindled a small fire, being careful that the sparks could not fly to ignite the acres of stained and matted hay, and opened a can of soup. She poured the contents into the iron kettle to simmer. Why, the empty can was another receptacle, wasn't it? And wouldn't each emptied can be an additional receptacle? "We can imagine they're porcelain cups," she thought. And, suddenly more cheerful, she began ladling out the warm liquid and speeding Mrs. Fales and the orderlies forth to the famishing.

It was a weird sight: Clara bending over her kettle, while up and down the hill flitted the yellow glint of lanterns, pausing and darting in the cavernous blackness of the night, as food was spooned into the mouths of prostrate men.

Dawn had its complications. The Confederate cavalry was glimpsed through the trees; the growl of guns indicated that the battle was now less distant. With the earliest streaking of the horizon, the wagons loomed again. But the train did not come for its scheduled (and so pitiful!) freight. By noon, the wounded were jumbled with the dead or dying in direst confusion. The afternoon was sultry and clouded; at six o'clock rain fell in torrents.

Fearing the effect of the rain, Clara hastened to cover the living with whatever was handy—blankets, coats, scraps of canvas, papers, remnants of pasteboard cartons, even the hay which she scooped up from the ground. She saw that to coax a fire to burn tonight would be a magician's trick; an inspection of the baggage car showed her also that her stock, which she had thought so bountiful, was running low. Three thousand diners are a good many! Yet still they came, by the wagonload.

What was the matter with the train? Mrs. Fales borrowed a mule, mounted and loped off five miles along the track to locate a telegraph wire. Then, when she had returned, when they had almost despaired, the little locomotive shrilled its whistle and chugged up to the siding. Through the wet night and far into the morning, the routine of moving the stretchers to the cars continued. But the outlook was brightened somewhat by the arrival of a second train and then a third.

Finally, on Tuesday afternoon, the hill slope yielded up the last of its occupants. Mrs. Fales, the Sanitary Commissioner, the orderlies, huddled onto a flatcar and left. And Clara rode back toward Alexandria in her own conveyance, which now was empty of all supplies, but was crowded with human wreckage.

After Bull Run, the Union troops were in full retreat. They gained the comparative safety of Washington and made a stand. But would the city be taken by the Southerners? Probably nothing averted that except the fact that Lee's army had been terribly reduced in numbers by the steady combat. Lee seized the Federal wagon trains, prepared to cross the Potomac—and struck fiercely at Chantilly.

It was three o'clock in the morning, and Clara, in her improvised refuge in a copse of poplars, descried a lantern threading through the trees. A man materialized from the shadows.

"Miss Barton, they told me I'd find you here. I am Dr. Brown. I've been patching up a lad over there at my post on the cliff. He can't survive and is, I guess, in no worse straits than hundreds of his mates. But he is hysterically calling for his sister—and something about that has got under my hide! The other doctors with me, even the other patients, all feel that we want to ease his distress. Will you speak to him?"

"Yes, of course. I daresay my people can wait a moment."

She glanced about her at the ground strewn with disheveled figures.

"I know you have more than your share of casualties. I would not ask if it weren't an urgent thing."

Beside Dr. Brown, guided by his lantern, Clara walked what seemed a long way, up a lane where they had to tread warily so that they might not trample the inevitable and abject rows of the mutilated. They came to a lighted place. A boy lay on a pallet of straw. The upper half of his uniform had been ripped off and his torso thickly bound with linen. His face was agonized, and constantly he tossed his head and mumbled, "Mary, Mary!"

Clara hesitated. "Put out the lantern," she said. "Let me be alone with him." Then, when the light had been extinguished and Dr. Brown had stepped aside, she knelt and slipped her arms about the boy's shoulders. He raised his hand, touched the soft lace of her collar, her hair—

"*Mary!* I was sure you'd hear me! Oh, Mary!"

She leaned and kissed his cheek, but said nothing. She pulled the blanket up around his feet. He was shivering, his lips blanched. She shrugged out of her shawl and threw that over him. After a while he relaxed.

Dr. Brown came, whispering through the darkness. "Has he—"

"No," Clara said. "He's sleeping."

"No hope for him, alas. If you want to go back—"

"Not yet. He may waken."

The doctor tiptoed away.

Clara was seated upright, with no support for her arms. Yet even in this numbing attitude she dozed. When she opened her eyes, the sun was glimmering in the east. She looked down. The boy was staring up into her face.

"Who are you?" he demanded, puzzled.

"My name is Clara Barton."

He stirred, and winced. "Last night I thought you were my sister. I suppose I was dreaming."

"You're much better this morning."

"Yes, I am. I was so cold, freezing. But now I'm warm. Where'd you come from?"

"I'm a nurse. I was over yonder."

"Have you been sitting here all the time?"

"It was only a few hours."

"Gee!" He pondered. "I suppose I'm in a bad fix. Will they ship me to a hospital?"

"Probably." She wished she might say it with more certainty, but he was, indeed, in a bad fix, and she knew the rules for hospitalization. Those who seemed doomed were often resigned to their doom.

"Miss Barton, they've got to send me back. I'm Hugh Johnson from New York City. My mother didn't want me to enlist, but I swore on a stack o' Bibles that the Rebels couldn't kill me, I'd get home. And I *must*. Or if not that, then I must get to Washington where my folks can come to me. Even if only to die! That was the thing my mother dreaded most, that I might die and she'd never know it. Please, Miss Barton! The train must be nearly ready. Get me on it!"

"Hush." She saw that the hysteria of the night might again engulf him. "You lie quietly, and I'll do what I can about it."

She settled him on his wretched pallet and walked down to the track. The train was being loaded. She went to the surgeon in charge. "I've a boy for you, sir. Hugh Johnson, Dr. Brown's patient."

"Shot through the abdomen, isn't he?" The surgeon shook his head. "A mortal wound. I'm sorry, Miss Barton. We have room for just the men who are expected to recover."

"You must take him, Doctor."

"No, it's out of the question."

"Can you guarantee the recovery of every man on this train?"

"I wish I could, God knows! But—"

"Hugh Johnson must go to Washington. I believe he will live. And I insist."

The surgeon looked at her. A month ago she had been a private citizen. She was that now, but somehow she had become a person of authority, too.

"Very well, Miss Barton," said the surgeon.

That day she spent feeding the injured as they were hauled from the field, before they were deposited by the wagons. She had devised this scheme as a more rapid system of doling out rations. Because she had devoted so much time to Hugh Johnson, she worked with redoubled vigor. The provost marshal strode up, saluted, and said that he had fifty prisoners, banished from the front line for some minor breach of discipline.

"They're not rascals, ma'am. Just young and— Well, you know how kids are. I thought maybe you could use 'em."

"I can." Fifty youngsters? She could have wept for sheer joy. And there at the platform were flatcars and a steaming engine.

By three o'clock Chantilly had been salvaged, the trains started from the battle zone, and Clara announced that the prisoners would have their own lunch. They had been gallant and obedient, she said. She was grateful to them, and she had a crate of canned goods which they must divide.

That was a queer sort of feast, offered under an ominously gray sky. Before it had well commenced, a storm crashed over them, lightning forked through the clouds, thunder reverberated. And at the same instant a bombardment sounded. The Confederates were at it again!

The uproar was deafening; the ear could not distinguish between heaven's wrath and earth's. The air vibrated, the turf shook beneath the feet. Thunderclaps, and volley after volley of cannon; thick darkness crisscrossed by flares of stark illumination athwart the trees' gnarled and dripping branches, on the scarred hills, the rocks, and the railroad track. And even when the storm abated, the guns dinned on.

At midnight the provost marshal popped up from somewhere.

"I'll look after my men, Miss Barton. I got a little Sibley tent and had it pitched for you. It's in the hollow. You'll not get out o' here before morning. Might as well try to sleep."

The hollow was slippery with mud, water washed under the tent's sides, and rain leaked in silvery cascades from the ceiling. There was no cot, not even a campstool, but the provost had folded a sodden blanket on a small box. Here, presumably, she was to rest her head. She sat down on the ground, selecting a spot which, though certainly not dry, was not a puddle. "If I slept," she thought, "the water would run into my ears and drown me." But her eyelids drooped.

At dawn, a single fife wafted a plaintive refrain. Clara jumped up. Was that the signal for retreat? She listened. Did she hear a drum, the beat of marching feet? She went out. No one was in view, except an officer cantering from the vicinity of the poplar copse.

"Miss Barton! Is anyone with you?"

"Apparently not." She gestured.

"We are retreating. Can you ride, if I get a horse for you?"

"Yes. But won't there be wounded?"

"They'll be brought. The enemy cavalry is skirting the hills."

"Tether the horse in the copse, Captain. I'll stay an hour or two."

"Aren't you afraid?"

"Yes," she said, "awfully. But I think I must stay and finish my job."

The fife, the drum, the regiments approached. Ragged, defeated men, dragging back from Chantilly. She watched them, tended their hurts.

The captain reined in. "You can't risk another hour, Miss Barton. The enemy is breaking over the hills. Follow the track to the next station. The train is there. Your horse is waiting. But I had no saddle."

"Don't bother about that!"

She ran to the poplars, loosened the bridle, swung up astride the horse. She slapped his flank and galloped for the track, clattered pell-mell along it, over the ties and cinders, and reached the train at last. The conductor stood behind the end coach, a flaming torch in his hand.

"Hurry!" he shouted. "Get on!"

As she stumbled up the steps and into the coach, the conductor flung the torch into a towering heap of combustible material in the station yard. Then he, too, scrambled aboard.

When the train rounded a curve, Clara looked back. The station was all ablaze; a troop of Confederate cavalry was dashing down the hill.

She visited Armory Square Hospital in Washington on the following Friday. Tracing the chaplain's record for the names of men for whom she had been especially concerned, she found the name of Hugh Johnson of New York.

"He is alive?"

"Yes," the chaplain said. "His mother and his sister Mary have been with him for two days."

"Did he know them?"

"Oh, yes. He is quite conscious. The doctors think he may get well."

...

13

O N SEPTEMBER 12, at Harpers Ferry, the Union attempted an offensive—and was rebuffed. Washington was distracted with the news. When and where would there be an end to these disappointments? Lee was at the threshold of the capital, and only the exceptional person could take encouragement from the fact that, at least, the brigades were no longer retreating.

After dinner on Saturday, the thirteenth, Clara went to her storeroom. A bit of paper drifted over the doorsill. She stooped and read:

"Harpers Ferry, not a moment to be lost."

The missive was unsigned. Clara pondered as to who could have penned it. Some doctor, perhaps? Some military nabob? Or Mrs. Fales? But it was not essential that she know.

Half an hour later she was in the office of Major Rucker of the quartermaster corps.

"Major, I want to go to Harpers Ferry. May I?"

"Maybe so." He was genial because he knew now what she could do. But he was dubious. "You'll have to have a wagon."

"Yes. No other vehicle could get me over the roads."

"I might ferret out a wagon somewhere, Miss Barton."

"Not *might*, Major. Say you *will*." She marveled at her own temerity.

"In the morning?"

"Yes. I'll be ready."

The wagon, high and wide, with a canopy of white canvas, looked like a huge, sprawling turtle; hitched to it were eight frisky little mules. The driver was a red-haired, red-bearded giant named Pete. Clara knew at sight that Pete was worth his weight in gold. Seated in the wagon bed were two of Major Rucker's men, and at the rear wheels were two more soldiers, each straddling a mule.

When the load of supplies had been settled, Clara got inside. She was wearing a plain print skirt and a snug alpaca jacket. Bonnetless, she had pinned a gypsy-striped silk scarf around her hair. She would have no change of clothing, but she had remembered to tie up a few toilet articles and some clean handkerchiefs in a bundle which could be wadded into her pocket.

Pete jerked the single rein by which he managed his little animals, and the equipage rattled into Pennsylvania Avenue. It was Sunday—"It always is," thought Clara, "and always I take off while decent folk are going to church in their best attire."

All day they drove, over stones and dikes, up and down the Maryland countryside. At nightfall, Pete turned into an open pasture where they camped. An indistinct artillery barrage could be heard, yet Clara's party cooked and ate a substantial supper and then slept soundly, the men wrapped in their blankets under the trees, Clara in the wagon. By dawn they were again on their way.

They did not have the road to themselves, but were wedged into a train of moving wagons, a column nearly ten miles in length, the ammunition and food for an army in battle. And, eddying on the sides of this solid column, were ranks of sick or incapacitated soldiers, who marched in the opposite direction toward temporary relief. As hour by hour these men straggled past, Clara busied herself in cutting loaves of bread and handing the slices over the wheel to eagerly grasping hands. At each little village she entered, she bought all the bread its inhabitants would sell, that her barrels and boxes might be replenished.

They came into a rocky glen, where rocks frowned above them and tall oaks shut out the sun. Pete pulled out of the road and braked his wagon.

"They fought there three days ago," he said, over his shoulder. "But now they've gone."

He spoke accurately. Jumping down, Clara surveyed the trampled ground, the crags blackened with powder smoke, the riddled groves. A place of horrible memories, deserted but for ghosts, silent but for the breeze in the oaks' branches. She sighed and got back into her seat.

"Shall I drive on, Miss?" Pete queried.

"Yes. There's cannonading—which means a fight somewhere."

At South Mountain they saw what was becoming familiar: rows of wounded laid out in a meadow. Clara stopped and, with her helpers, ministered to them. But many were beyond assistance. All too soon she had adjusted the last bandage and need not linger.

She had her foot on the step when she saw a herd of cattle winding toward her up the road and, riding behind it, several uniformed horsemen led by a lieutenant.

"Rations for our troops," said Pete. "Hey, Miss, the officer's wavin'. I b'lieve he wants to talk to you."

The lieutenant trotted forward. "Miss Barton?" He touched his cap, lowered his voice. "May I say something to you, confidentially?"

She nodded, surprised as much at the troubled expression on his face as at his words.

"That house up ahead, the one behind the fence. Would you suppose that it was tenanted?"

Clara looked as he pointed. "No, the shutters are tight."

"It *is*, though. Twenty-five wounded Confederates are in there, lost from their own people, hiding. They're in desperate shape, almost starving. A moment ago, a man in civilian clothes accosted me. He is the doctor who has been caring for them. He begged me for two of these cows. Milk, he said, would save a dozen lives." The lieutenant paused. "Miss Barton, before this war I was a divinity student at Harvard, learning the brotherhood of man. Now I am a bonded officer and responsible for government property in my charge. And the cows are government property. What can I do?"

Clara smiled. "You can do nothing except your duty. But," she said, "I am neither bonded nor responsible. Ride on, Lieutenant."

His eyes sought hers, and then he too smiled. Bowing, he spurred his horse ahead. When the cattle and their herders were out of sight, two fat cows were trailing Clara's wagon. She turned to the soldier on his mule at the rear wheel.

"Sergeant Field, we can't be encumbered by these straying beasts. Drive them to that house, the one with the shuttered windows, and put them inside the fence. And be sure to bar the gate. I shouldn't want them to stray again."

The increase of stragglers seemed alarming to Clara. It indicated that the army lacked not only physical strength but spirit also. "Though why shouldn't they feel depressed?" she thought. "Always defeated, always retreating. Well, *I* shan't be demoralized."

It was noon; traffic had choked the road, the column was at a standstill. Pete slipped nosebags of oats over the muzzles of his mules and then walked back to peep under the canvas flap.

"You happy, Miss?"

"No," Clara said, "I'm not. Pete, I've made a discovery. The traveling order of a supply train is all wrong. Here we are, stuck behind the ammunition conveyances, the trucks of food and clothing for the active troops. Our supplies will be among the first needed if there's a battle in front of us—and I don't doubt there is, or will be. Yet, as we're going now, we shall be two or three days moving up to it. And that will be too late for real service, just as we were too late at Harpers Ferry and South Mountain. We must short-circuit the ordinary military methods and travel behind the artillery."

"Can't be done, Miss Barton." Pete grinned. (It would be interesting to know what he was thinking of her then.) "You might as well try to rearrange the stars in the sky as swap places in this parade."

"It can be done," she said. "By strategy. You follow my instructions and I'll show you."

Her instructions, which Pete followed, were to swerve out of the column before sunset. When the mules had been unhitched, Clara and the men ate an early supper and went immediately to sleep. At one o'clock, she got them up. "Harness," she said. "We're stealing the march on everybody else." By starlight, in the night's stillness, Clara's wagon trundled past the others, past the camps of their slumbering drivers, and gained ten miles and was in advance of the ammunition, even abreast of the artillery.

So she rode across the Potomac, through the quaint hamlet of Sharpsburg, over Antietam Creek, and into the fertile bowl which was to be the scene of one of history's great battles.

The poet Whittier has said that two days before, at Frederick, meagerly distant, old Barbara Frietche had rescued a sacred flag which Stonewall Jackson fired upon:

> "In her attic window the staff she set,
> To show that one heart was loyal yet."

Clara stood on a grassy knoll, binocular raised to her eyes. Behind her was a farmhouse and a barn and acres of ripening corn. She looked into an arena in which were two armies, one hundred and sixty thousand men. It was ten o'clock, and there had been preliminary skirmishing. Joe Hooker, "Fighting Joe of Massachusetts," had sallied forth and been overborne. Now other units bombarded, the infantry lined up under cover of the barking ordnance.

The barn would be Clara's haven; the corn was tall, almost concealing it, separating it from the house where the surgeons were in possession. When she had unpacked her boxes (sent here from zealous, prayerful women in Vermont, New Hampshire, every Northern and Middle Western state) and had readied the barn, Clara went to the house to appraise its condition. Arms full of parcels—cotton, quilts, stimulants—she elbowed through the farmyard gate.

A man was on the porch, Dr. Dunn of Conneautville, Pennsylvania. She had met him before, at Bull Run.

"Clara Barton! Do my senses deceive me or is it actually you? And what have you? Not bandages! Then God has indeed remembered us! We've torn up the last sheet in this house, we haven't a rag, a lint, a swab of gauze. On tables inside are four etherized patients—and we had thought we must use green corn leaves in the amputations!" He took the things from her. "Will you remain with us?"

"No, Dr. Dunn," she said. "My place is with my little band in the barn. It's rapidly filling."

"There'll be terrific slaughter today, Miss Barton."

"I am afraid so," she said.

Three times during the day the ground around the house and barn was contested, and danger was so very close that Clara was deafened by the noise of exploding shells. Smoke whirled in hot, sulphurous blasts to parch her lips and sting her eyes and nostrils. Nothing in her previous experience paralleled this. She never had been so rushed—or thought she could be. It was unnecessary for Pete and Sergeant Field and her other helpers to go far in search of the wounded, for they were all about, hundreds of them, at the barn door, dropping in the corn. At moments, the walls of the building were only a treacherous shelter. As Clara bent to hold a cup of water to the mouth of one poor, thirsty fellow, a bullet whined through the barn, clipped a hole in her sleeve and knocked the cup from her hand. She sprang back, shuddering.

She saw a man just inside the door, a newcomer, and paused to inquire the extent of his wounds.

"I'm not much hurt. Only this bump on my cheek. What is it, lady?"

"A shot," she said. "Lodged against the jawbone."

"It burns like crazy! Will you take it out for me?"

"No. But the surgeon will. Go over to the house—"

"I've been," he said. "They're busy there with worse hurts than mine. I'm Shea; corporal." He displayed the stripe on his sleeve. "Please lance my cheek!"

"I can't. I have no lance."

"You've got a pocketknife, though." Another soldier who had been lying near the corporal was inching now along the floor toward Clara. "I'm Eaton, ma'am, orderly sergeant of

Illinois, reporting—and not so much battered up, either. A couple o' smashed ankles, but my hands are all right." Sergeant Eaton crawled closer. "Shea's my buddy. I'll grip his head. Where's that pocketknife and your nerve?"

Slowly Clara drew the little knife from her apron. The blade was sharp and clean—

"Gosh!" Shea said. "I feel better a'ready! You're something of a doc yourself, lady."

"She's Clara Barton," said Sergeant Eaton. "I recognized her."

At dusk Pete came to her with the disconcerting word that there was no more bread. "*Or* crackers, Miss. I reckon we've fed upward of a thousand since noon. What'll we do?"

"The unopened boxes of wine?"

"I've got three. Been saving 'em back—for snake bite, maybe."

"This *is* snake bite, Pete. This is an extremity. Open them. And tell Sergeant Field to light some lanterns and set them about."

He turned away. The next instant, startled by his astonished ejaculation, Clara hastened and saw that these few precious bottles of wine had been packed not in sawdust but in finely sifted Indian meal.

"Enough for gallons of gruel!" She was jubilant. "Oh, Pete, I'd rather have this meal than gold or rubies! Build a fire behind the barn. I know there must be kettles in the farmhouse kitchen. I'll fetch them. We'll soon have food fit for a king."

She ran up the narrow path to the house, onto the porch. How dark it was here! She went in. Dr. Dunn was sitting at the kitchen table. The flicker of a sputtering candle showed his face haggard and stern.

"You're tired, Doctor."

He looked up at her. "Yes, I'm tired," he said savagely. "Tired of such negligence, such carelessness on the part of my superiors. I have here five hundred grievously injured men who must be vigilantly tended if they're to live. And that two inches of tallow candle is all the light I have, or can get. When it's out, my work and the work of the other surgeons will stop. How am I to endure this situation?"

"My barn is well lighted. Your house will be also."

"What's that?" He rose, staring.

"Yes. I brought ten extra lanterns and I have plenty of candles. I'll trade them to you for some kettles. A fair exchange is no robbery, Dr. Dunn."

It occurred to her to go down into the cellar under the kitchen, and there she found three barrels of wheat flour and a sack of salt. She was rich! She could have wept for gratitude. With Pete's fire burning brightly, she mixed water and meal for gruel. She made slabs of hardtack to be baked in the embers. The kettles boiled and bubbled; the browning flour gave off a delicious odor. All that night Sergeant Field and his crew carried warm food to the hungry and suffering.

Antietam! Clara would never forget it. When at length the engagement was over, it was rated as a victory for the North. A dearly bought victory and not decisive. Nevertheless, it marked the flood tide of the Confederates' force. After that there was a gradual diminishing.

David Barton visited Washington and presented himself unannounced at her door.

"Clara, I've enlisted."

"Oh, David!" She embraced him, gave him a chair. He was so well, brawny and muscular as he'd been when a boy. His eyes gleamed, his face was weathered, his hair and beard grizzled. She thought he was the handsomest man in the world. "Oh, David!"

"I felt I had to. And, of course, I wanted to. My fifteen-year-old son is an army courier and telegrapher. Everyone's in, everyone who hasn't the most pressing reasons for staying out. And I hadn't. Julia can competently handle my business, and there's ample money for her and my girls. Are you sorry, Sis?"

"I suppose I'm not, really. I know how you feel. But I hate war. More and more I hate it!"

"You've seen the havoc."

"Yes. And I hate the drivel people write about it, David. Disguising it in pretty language. War is an octopus, squeezing the good out of everything, swallowing everybody up!"

He chuckled. "It'll not swallow me up. Or down. I'm old—and tough. What was it Father said once about the fiber of the Bartons?" He paused rather abruptly, and added, "Have you heard from Stephen?"

"No. I think of him all the time. I've dispatched messages, hoping one would be smuggled through somehow. And I shan't quit hoping! An infantryman, Sergeant Farley, told me to depend on him. And I shall."

"Good for you!" David patted her shoulder. "I think about *you* all the time, Clara. Mustn't exhaust yourself. You're doing so much."

"It's very little, in fact." She shook her head. "I have a dream of what might be accomplished if only the rules of warfare could be revised, if some unified and concerted effort at improvement could be made. As they are now, the rules are barbaric. But then war, every phase of it, is barbaric anyway. Talk to me of home, David."

For a tranquil interval he talked lovingly to her of home.

14

IN DECEMBER, after an autumn of trailing the troops through Maryland and into Virginia, Clara went to Falmouth, where a large portion of the Army of the Potomac was encamped on the Rappahannock River overlooking Fredericksburg. For this expedition Major Rucker had allotted her six wagons and an ambulance. She had eight men to accompany her, but the ruddy, good-humored Pete had been transferred elsewhere—and Clara missed him. That the eight were civilians rather than soldiers, hucksters and mule breakers hired by the government as drivers, she knew. She was to learn that they could be both sullen and fractious.

It was winter, very cold, and Clara rode in the ambulance, shielded by the buttoned-down canvas roof. On the first day out from Washington, at four o'clock in the afternoon, her conveyance was pulled into a little gully and halted. Glancing out, she saw that all the wagons had been formed into a circle, the mules unhitched, the men had dismounted and were raking up sticks and dried grass, as if for a fire.

But why should they have stopped? She called to the ambulance driver, George, who seemed to be the leader of the squad.

"Night," George said laconically. "We ain't owls."

"You have two hours more of daylight. You can go on that long."

126

"We only drive," George stated, "when we feel like it."

She was somewhat taken aback. "I think," she said, "you drive when *I* feel like it. And I feel like it now. We'll go on."

He regarded her insolently a minute, then strolled to his friends in the center of the circle. Clara had withdrawn behind the curtains, but she could see that a consultation was in progress. There were mutterings and grumbled curses and much cracking of the teamsters' whips. Presently the mules were put into the shafts and the caravan jolted again onto the road.

Clara smiled to herself and thought that the tiff, such as it was, had been settled. But then she was not so positive, for the two hours elapsed, the sun sank, darkness came on. It was six o'clock, and seven, and eight—and George drove on as though he meant never to stop! His behavior was that of a perverse child. His rigid back and the tilt of his cap seemed to say, "Well, if you're so fond of this, you shall have an abundance!"

"And he *is* a child," thought Clara. "An impudent bully. I've had his kind in my classes. He wants me to ask him to stop. I'll not do it."

She was beginning to be hungry, and she knew that George and his fellows must be, too. But she said nothing. Finally, after nine-thirty, with a prodigious squealing of brakes, the wheels were stilled.

Clara got down. She was chilled through, stiff from her cramped attitude, a little apprehensive of what the night might hold. But she had mapped her course of action. She laid a fire. The men lounged near by, making no pretense of helping. She hung a stewpan on a spit and heated soup. She fried eggs and bacon. She had no table, but she spread a cloth upon the ground and set it neatly with plates, forks, and spoons. She opened a glass of crabapple jelly, a jar of blackberry jam, and placed them in the middle of the cloth. She brewed a huge pot of coffee. The men were watching. Each of them had his own food box containing eight days' rations of salted meat and bread. They unfastened the lids of their boxes, looked in —and then at the attractive prospect of Clara's luxurious fare.

"Gentlemen," Clara said, "supper is served."

They came reluctantly, one at a time, edging up, sheepishly taking plates and the cups of coffee which she poured. When all were seated, Clara sat down with them and began to chat casually. Probably she had never indulged in more difficult conversation than that, for there were few responses, but she could not doubt that the supper was appreciated. They ate largely, grunting and casting funny sidelong glances at their amiably smiling hostess.

As the last morsel vanished, Clara collected the dishes, washed them and stowed them away. The fire had dwindled to a bed of coals lighting the surrounding trees with a rosy and almost theatrically beautiful glow. As if by common consent, the drivers had sauntered into the shadows, out of sight. Had she not heard occasionally the guttural rumble of their voices, Clara might have thought they were gone for good.

After a while, and just as she had turned toward her blankets in the ambulance, George emerged.

"Miss Barton?" With the firelight on his black hair and eyes, his rugged countenance and burly, rough-clad figure, he looked sinister as a bandit. The other seven were at his heels, like a bandit's cohorts. "Miss Barton, we got something to say."

"Well," Clara said, "that's fine. Come up where you'll be warm and comfortable, George."

He came a pace closer. "The thing is, we think mebbe we've been—mistaken. None of us ever seen a wagon train bossed by a lady before, an' we didn't hanker ever to see one. When we found out that you was in charge of this'n, we was mad. We thought we'd act mean an' contrary, an' bust it up. But— Miss Barton, that was the best grub I've et in two years! An' you called us *gentlemen*."

"Why not? You are gentlemen, and I shall always treat you as such. I can understand your feeling about being directed by a woman, but in these dreadful days we all have to do things we don't just fancy. I think you'll become accustomed to me. In fact, since you approve of my cooking, I think we shall get along splendidly together and be fast friends. It would be too bad if we weren't, wouldn't it? Because we may have a big job facing us. Good night, George. I'm going to bed now."

She started for the ambulance. But George, the gentleman, was before her, hurrying to assist her, rolling a keg into position for her to step upon, buttoning the canvas down once she was inside.

"I'll mend the fire, Miss Barton. Don't you fret about it. An' me an' the boys will sleep right here. If you should want us, all you got t' do is holler."

Next morning, Clara was awakened by a succession of muffled sounds. She lifted the curtain and peeped out at great activity. The men were bustling about, spreading the cloth on the ground, setting out dishes. The fire crackled blithely, the mules were hitched. George was walking up from the creek, a bucket in his hand.

"This is for the boss," he asserted. "Don't none o' you touch it. An' pipe down that infernal yawpin' or you'll be sorry! I know about ladies, even if you don't. They got to get their beauty sleep. Gosh! Mebbe we'll have flapjacks for breakfast."

At Falmouth, Clara was established in the Lacy House, an old mansion of magnificent architecture and landscaped gardens, abandoned now by its owner, and within a stone's throw of the Rappahannock. From the piazza, she could see the muddy, ice-bordered river, with the town of Fredericksburg on the far side, and, on the Falmouth shore, a city of tents wherein Union soldiers awaited the command to storm Fredericksburg. There was no bridge over the water. When the command, long anticipated and often postponed, should be issued, a pontoon bridge must be constructed.

The Lacy House had twelve spacious rooms, all empty now except for Miss Barton and her small staff. Clara devoutly wished that they might always be so, that there would never be a battle to fill them with pain and horror—and knew that the wish was vain. This dreadful drama of a nation in travail must play itself out to the end; and already, in the North, certain people were criticizing General Burnside for his delay. "Cross that river!" said newspaper editorials. "Occupy those brick houses on the other bank! What if it is winter? This is war!" Still Burnside hesitated.

Then on a day of hazy, moderate weather, the engineers began working with the pontoons, lashing the boats, flinging down planks and timber. Above, on the Fredericksburg heights, was the stirring of suspense, as the Confederates girded themselves to defend.

From the portico Clara saw the first Union squads march out upon the bridge, to be mowed down by batteries of hidden cannon. She saw the second venture and heard General Burnside's shout, "Bring the guns to bear. We'll shell them out!" Clara left the portico then, for musketry made a fiendish clamor. Bullets whizzed, windows in the Lacy House were crashing and splintering. The engineers were furiously trying to complete the span of pontoons, despite the enemy's scything.

They did it at last, and their troops trotted over to the far shore, where men in gray were swarming out of every building in Fredericksburg, surging through every street, solidifying into a wall of rifles and artillery along the Rappahannock's cliffs. This was the battle.

In the midst of it, a courier scuttled into the Lacy House. He had a penciled scrap of crumpled paper for Clara: "Come to me. Your place is here."

"Who gave you this?"

"A doctor, ma'am," the courier said. "He's got a little hospital rigged up in a vacant building."

"Very well." She grabbed her medicine kit.

But George had planted himself in her path. "No, Miss Barton."

"What are you saying, George?" she asked impatiently.

"You can't go."

"Oh, nonsense." She shoved at his detaining arm. "Let me go!"

"No, I won't. Not alone—"

"Go with me then."

His black eyes widened. He gasped. "Me? Into that—that— I don't like it! I swore I'd never get messed up with no fighting. You think I'm a danged fool? I'm not!"

"Well, I am. Stand aside, George."

He groaned. "Oh, all *right*. Let's start! An' you boys bring the wagon," he yelled to his seven henchmen.

The bridge rocked under their hurrying feet; shot hissed into the water around them. As they ascended the Fredericksburg bank, a sniper's bullet tore away George's coattail and hurled him backward. Clara looked over her shoulder. He was paddling grotesquely, like a walrus.

"George!"

"Go on!" he yelled. "Run. I can swim. I'll catch up with you."

Within fifteen minutes, Clara was at the doctor's "little hospital" and diving into her kit for splints and linen. There George found her. Except for being soaking wet, he was none the worse for his icy bath.

The days and weeks spent at Falmouth were different from anything she had known, for now she had the cold to contend with. Snow and sleet fell; often the men picked up were partially frozen and must be thawed before they could be bandaged. Clara kept fires on every hearth in the big house, tea and broth always simmering on the kitchen stoves. She wrapped hot bricks in rags with which to warm the cots and straw pallets. The rooms soon were overflowing, even though wagons plied steadily toward the railroad which took the more hopeful cases to Washington. Besides nursing, Clara also had the responsibility of supervising the orderlies, and every few hours she must cross into Fredericksburg for those injured detailed to her by the surgeons.

On one of these sorties, she stood on the curb to watch a regiment of infantrymen tramping through the street toward the front line on the heights. As always, she was touched by the sight. How young they were, how browned and vigorous. And how many would be so tomorrow?

An officer, glimpsing her, pulled up his horse, bent from his saddle. "Madam, you are within the range of a thousand rifles, in terrible peril! What on earth are you doing here? Do you want protection?"

She smiled up at him. "No, General. I believe I am the best-protected woman in the United States."

A pert little corporal had overheard. "That's so!" he bellowed, and cheered lustily. "Ain't that so?" "*What's* so?" someone cried. "Ain't she the best-protected woman in the United States?" The cheer echoed to the next rank, through all the ranks. "*That's* so!"

"I believe," said the blinking general, baring his head, "you are right, madam."

Two Confederate prisoners were brought to the Lacy House, one a lieutenant of cavalry, the other an eighteen-year-old private; both seemed to have the chance to survive. Clara bedded them side by side in an alcove. She felt a special pity for the boy. His name was Donald, his home in a Georgia village.

"Am I going to die?" he queried as she sponged his face.

"Oh, no. You have a nasty saber gash, but it will heal, Donald."

"What *will* become of me?"

"I imagine you'll be sent to some Northern camp and, after the war's over, exchanged for a Union man who is now a Confederate prisoner."

"Who'll tell my family?" He stared at her. "What if I die in that Northern camp? My mother and my dad, they'll wait— and what if they never know? That would be mighty hard on 'em."

"Yes, it would." She thought a minute. "I live in Washington. I'll give you my address. Whatever happens, whatever they do with you, you'll surely be allowed to write to me, Donald. Then I'll communicate with your family."

His eyes brightened—and were dour again. "How could you? The mails are out."

"When we're at peace once more, the mails will be resumed.

But if they shouldn't be— Well, there'll be some way for me to notify your parents."

"Gosh! I hope so. Uncertainty can be crueler than out-and-out bad news, Miss Barton." As she rose, the basin in her hands, he murmured, " 'When we're at peace.' I like the sound o' that. But will it ever be true? Will we ever have peace?"

"Yes," she said. "That's one thing we can count on, Donald. We must live for that."

On the day that Clara had twelve hundred people under the roof of the Lacy House, she told George that she regretted the amount of furniture which the previous occupants had left behind them. "These chairs and whatnots and taborets. They're beautiful. But not *useful*. We're all cluttered up with them."

George had an excellent idea. Why not dismember the superfluous things and use the wood to convert the corner cupboards into tiers of bunks? He got hammer and saw and built the tiers, and also more bunks in the halls, under the tables, over the beds, and on the stair landings. Even so, the nurses must step cautiously lest they jostle an arm or a leg in splints.

Whenever Clara's fortitude seemed almost to ebb away, some incident would ensue to spur her on—and one such incident was the coming of Mrs. Fales.

"Well, Miss Barton?" She strode in, her old hat cocked at a ridiculous angle. "I got here. By hook or crook."

"Oh, Mrs. Fales!" Joy was in Clara's ejaculation.

"How are things? What shall I do first?" She tied on her apron. At noon, she said, "There's a poor child downstairs. Shot through the lungs. His breathing's shallow, he can't last long. He's sitting on the floor, straight as a ramrod against the wall. I asked an orderly to move him. But he said no, he wouldn't be touched. And he wants a milk punch."

"I'll mix the punch," Clara said. "We have fresh milk and eggs and brandy."

As she spooned the frothy beverage between the boy's lips, Clara asked him his name.

"Riley Faulkner," he gasped. "Ohio. Ashtabula County."

She thought, with Mrs. Fales, that he could not draw those tortured inhalations much longer. But in the evening he was still breathing.

"And stronger," said Mrs. Fales. "I wouldn't have believed it if I hadn't seen with my own eyes."

Next morning Mrs. Fales announced, "That Faulkner boy may pull through yet."

"He should be in a more accessible spot," Clara said.

"Not him. He won't budge. And he wants another milk punch."

"He shall have it!"

If there could have been a subject for joking in that grim place, Riley Faulkner of Ashtabula was such a phenomenon. For two solid weeks he was to sit there in his corner, not budging, growing always a bit stronger, always demanding milk punch. Even when he was finally persuaded to let the orderlies carry him on a stretcher to the Washington train, he had a bottle of his favorite drink tucked into his blouse under the blankets.

After a four-day truce, the batteries at Fredericksburg boomed again. On the morning of the fiercest fighting, when the Lacy House trembled to its foundations, the Confederate lieutenant gripped Clara's hand as she passed his cot.

"You've been kind to me, Miss Barton, and to my comrade,

the Georgia lad. You're rendering a stupendous service here. I entreat you not to cross the river today."

"Why not?"

"I can't tell you. But you must not go. Perhaps it is a disloyalty for me to say this much, and if so, I pray I may be pardoned. Please, please, Miss Barton, don't go!"

She thanked him—and went, as usual. She could not disappoint those who were expecting her.

At dusk she returned, knowing why the Confederate had warned her. A trap had been set for Burnside. When the trap was sprung, Burnside had been overwhelmed and Fredericksburg lost.

The South might be weakening. It was not yet conquered.

Clara alighted from a Washington streetcar, stumbled through the muddy street and up the flight of stairs to her apartment. The day was dreary and raw, late in January. She unlocked her door and just avoided falling over a wooden box which stood in the center of the floor. She slammed the door and, sitting down on the box, gazed around her at the chill, somewhat dirty room. How strange it seemed, this silence, after the months of noise and frenzied confusion of the Lacy House. She had the sensation of unreality—and she was weary to the marrow of her bones.

In a mirror on the opposite wall she saw herself, damp and bedraggled, bonnet awry, mantle and skirt shabby, shoes scuffed and unpolished.

"I look like a beggar," she thought. "A scarecrow. A wet hen. And I have no better clothes than these. Everything I own is in shreds."

And she had very little money either. Disconsolately she computed: her salary would be paid in February. But from that must be subtracted the sum with which she hired her substitute at the Patent Office. If she spent the remainder for clothing, she could not replenish her stores—not unless she drew further upon her savings, and she feared to do that.

She had not shed a tear in Fredericksburg or Falmouth. Now her composure dissolved. Somehow the deluge of weeping eased her. After a while she wiped her eyes, got up and struck a match to the gas jet. And then she noticed the box upon which she had been sitting.

It was addressed to her. Underneath her name was the intriguing word "Personal." What was in the box? She ran for a hatchet and pried loose the lid. Inside were folds of tissue and a card: FROM FRIENDS IN OXFORD. She lifted the paper—

Skirts, jackets, collars, handkerchiefs, shoes, boots, gloves! And petticoats, aprons, a knitted hood, stockings! An entire wardrobe, all for her, from her dear friends back home!

The tears welled again, but she smiled through them.

She wore the lovely new things that afternoon in February when she was summoned to the Lincoln Hospital. The messenger had been rather mysterious, she didn't know who wanted her, or why. She was told to go to Ward 17. Still baffled, she entered.

Seventy men were there, facing toward the door, saluting. Every one had been at Falmouth, every one her patient. A young chap, pink complexioned and husky looking, came and took her hand.

"Hello, Miss Barton. **Don't you** recognize me? I'm Faulkner."

"You're surely not!"

"Guess I was a skeleton when you coaxed me onto that train, eh? Well, I didn't die. And the milk punch lasted all the way to Washington."

15

I N THE spring of 1863, Clara was at Hilton Head Island, South Carolina. The intention of the Union just then was to blast Charleston both by land and from the sea, to regain Fort Sumter and the other four forts in Charleston harbor. The Northern army had a base on the island and already the ships of the United States Navy collected off the coast.

For three reasons Clara had wished to go to Hilton Head. The Army of the Potomac seemed now well provisioned—thanks, in a measure, to her own industry and donations. David, as an officer of the quartermaster department, was stationed there. And, best reason of all, there was the possibility that Stephen might not be far away, to be found, somehow, by his brother and sister. Besides, Clara thought that the trend of the war would soon be in this easterly direction, and surely there would be work for her here.

She sailed for Hilton Head in the transport *Arogo*. Warping to the dock on April 7, the *Arogo* was greeted by a salvo of cannon. Clara was told that the assault upon Charleston was scheduled for three o'clock of that very afternoon, and she felt that her arrival was most timely. But the assault was postponed. Within twenty-four hours, the brigades which had put out to sea were disembarking again and making camp.

"What had they returned for?" Clara queried in her journal.

"Conjecture was rife; all sorts of rumors. . . . The one general idea prevailed that the expedition had 'fizzled.' "

She was, indeed, entering upon a period of postponements and fizzling. For months she would be immured in inactivity. And for a while she rather liked the lull. She was warmly welcomed and comfortably housed here. Her reputation had preceded her. Nurses from the hospital called on her, a captain sent her flowers, a major serenaded her. One day she was publicly presented with a beautifully bound pocket Bible, the gift of the soldiers, and a speech was made extolling her virtues. Embarrassed, she noted in her journal, "I do not deserve such friends. And how *can* I deserve them?"

The conveniences of the island were many. The mails went regularly to New York. Clara had her own ambulance, horses, and drivers, all to be utilized when occasion should arise. And for this interval of balmy days and nights calm and mellow with tropical stars, she had a saddle horse to ride along the leafy bridle lanes. She read and wrote letters and had time for such communications as this, to David, "My clothes are as well washed as at home, and I have a house to iron in, if I had the iron. I could be as clean and sleek as a kitten. Don't you want a smooth sister enough to send her a flatiron?"

Evenings, the camp resounded with the singing voices of soldiers, and Clara, on the piazza of the barracks, would hear the choruses of that old chantey which was her favorite:

"Nicodemus the slave was of African birth
He was bought for a bagful of gold;
He was reckoned as part of the salt of the earth,
And he died years ago, very old.
'Twas the last word he said as we laid him away
In the stump of an old hollow tree,—

'Wake me up,' was his charge, 'at the first break of day,
Wake me up for the great jubilee.'
Then run and tell Elijah to hurry up, Pomp,
To meet us at the gum tree down in the swamp,
To wake Nicodemus today."

In fact, Hilton Head would have been altogether delightful
—if only Clara could have felt that she was doing her duty.
Instead, she thought she was much like the sleeping Nicodemus. Somewhere else the old conflict was being waged,
somewhere men perished because of deprivations. Here, by
contrast, the Sanitary Commission maintained a depot of stores
and seemed equal to the needs of the encampment. Since that
day when Clara first learned of it, the Commission had made
strides. Though still a private unit, it had become a strong
medium, co-operating with the Medical Corps and—by fairs,
bazaars, auctions, and other and often amusing devices—
raising large amounts of money with which to benefit the
soldiers. Clara Barton was not vital to the Commission's depot
at Hilton Head. She was an honored guest rather than a
worker. She might nurse a few cases of dysentery, and teach
classes of Negro boys to read, and buy fruits for finicky convalescents (and these things she did), but more and more as
the weeks passed, she felt that she was wasting herself upon
trivialities. She still had no news from Stephen. Perhaps she
was never to have any, and it was folly to wait. Oughtn't she
be again with what she designated as "my own army" in
Virginia?

Then in mid-July the North assailed Fort Wagner from
Morris Island. The battles continued in a sequence with in-
creasing severity.

Clara went at once to Morris Island. It was a stretch of sand hills, barren of trees, devoid of pure water, spotted with malarial marshes. Her post was opposite the fire from all the forts, inadequately shadowed by a sand dune. Walking, she sank to her ankles in sand. Frequent squalls whisked sand blindingly into her eyes. The sun was a demon, from which the only refuge was a floorless dog tent pitched in shifting sand.

Hour after hour she boiled water for drinking purposes and to wash wounds. She cooked cereals and eggs and fed the hungry. The siege was obstinate, from the land batteries and from the ships in the harbor. Charleston must capitulate! Fort Sumter was smashed to a crumble of sand and stone; Fort Gregg and Fort Wagner were regained; a cemetery grew to frightening size on Morris Island—

But Charleston was invincible. The siege failed.

Clara went back to Hilton Head. Now she was definitely restless. Ill for a while and then restored to health, she wondered if this horror would ever cease, if peace would ever come. She remembered what she had said to the little Confederate in Lacy House. How could she have been so positive that the war would some day be over?

In the West, along the Mississippi, General Grant was closing in on Rebel territory, holding with bulldog tactics the ground he seized. Perhaps the victory, if ever won, would hinge upon this domination of the West. In the East the armies were at stalemate, neither one able to strike a fatal blow. And in Washington, President Lincoln had issued the Emancipation Proclamation.

To be at Hilton Head at such a time seemed to Clara like dallying on the primrose path.

And one day David came to see her. He had received a letter from Stephen.

"Clara, it's that message of yours which you gave to Sergeant Farley. Finally, and by a roundabout way, it reached him."

"I thought it would! There was something in Sergeant Farley's manner—and he had luck charms, a four-leaf clover and a rabbit's foot."

"But Stephen refuses to do as you suggested. He hasn't been molested as yet and thinks he may not be. Better, he says, for him to stay where he is than to risk leaving. His Southern neighbors would certainly try to prevent that."

"Is he *safe,* David?"

"As safe as anyone is in this mad world. There's nothing more that we can do."

Clara meditated. "Then I'll not remain here. It isn't the place for me. I thank God that Stephen is alive. I pray he's acting wisely. Oh, I do wish we could have seen him, David."

"You're going to Virginia, Sis?"

"Yes, I may be of some use. But things are different now from what they were even a year ago. The Sanitary and the Christian commissions are distributing supplies. Other women are nursing in the field, many of them very efficiently, and hundreds more have volunteered for the army hospitals."

"Yes," David said. "Mr. Amos Bronson Alcott's daughter, for instance. Miss Louisa M. Alcott. She's a writer, I believe. She was at the Georgetown hospital last winter. Well, Clara, you could be appointed wherever you chose—if you're dissatisfied with being a lone wolf."

"Wolf?" She laughed. "Candidly, I wonder if perhaps I ought to have some official standing. Organization is the thing, David. I've always thought so. Centralized organization. People are good. If only their benevolence could be welded into an instrument!" She was sober now, sighing. "I can imagine it. But what can one person do?"

"More maybe than you know," said David.

Clara was absent from the battlefield until May of 1864. Then she was at Belle Plain on the Rappahannock, near Fredericksburg, where the injured were being brought from the struggles of the Wilderness and Spotsylvania.

She went by boat and, at the landing, stepped off upon a narrow cinder lane which protruded from a basin of mud. It was raining, had been raining for days. The soil was red clay, scraped to powder by ten thousand wheels and converted by the torrents to a vast mortar bed, glassy as a lake and much the color of brick dust. Through this gluey substance, six hundred wagons had plowed, hub deep, and stalled before they could reach the cinder ridge. Small boats were anchored and waiting, but from the look of things there would be an interminable period elapsing before they could take on their cargoes of the hospital-bound.

Some members of the Christian Commission were at Belle Plain. Most of them were totally unskilled workers, though aching to be of service. As Clara contemplated the doleful vista, a young clergyman stepped to her side.

"Madam, do you think the wagons are filled with the maimed?"

"I think they are, undoubtedly."

"They will scarcely get aboard the boats by nightfall!"

"I'm afraid not," she said.

"What can we do for them?"

"They're hungry and must be fed."

"Dear, dear!" His sensitive face clouded. "I am with the Christian Commission. We have books, magazines, so much good literature—"

"And food?"

"None," he said, "except crackers."

"I have coffee. Crackers and coffee are a meal!"

"But where shall we brew the coffee?" He gazed wistfully about at the wet hill flanking the ridge.

"There's a log," Clara said. "We'll build a fire behind it. This loose brush will burn if we stoke it with papers, your books and magazines."

"A fire?" He looked startled. "Just *here,* madam?"

"Just here, sir."

While she went to the boat for her kettles, the clergyman tussled with the brush and twigs. The good literature was invaluable for stoking and soon the coffee boiled.

"But, madam, our crackers are in barrels. We *cannot* carry the barrels to the wagons." His brow creased and he twiddled his slim, sooty fingers. "What can we do?"

"I have aprons. Oh, not exactly aprons, either, just rectangles of calico." She took one from her bag and pinned it over her frock, fastening the corners to her belt. She pinned another calico about the clergyman's waist, making a capacious pouch which she filled with crackers. "That's fine!" She handed him a kettle of coffee. "Come." She walked to the edge of the mud lake—and heard him speaking behind her.

"How—how are we to get *to* the wagons?"

"By wading. Of course, there's no other way."

"Wading? Oh—"

She lifted her skirt and stepped, up to her knees, into the mud. And after a minute he sloshed in, too, holding his kettle aloft, submitting manfully to this initiation into military life.

That was the day when Clara Barton's indignation drove her to an act of daring. By evening she had returned to Washington and had sent for a Senator whom she had known for years, the chairman of the Military Affairs Committee.

"The people of the neighborhood will not admit these 'dirty, lousy common soldiers' to their homes," she said, "and the army officers are not compelling them to do it. Therefore, the wounded lie out in the rain, because there aren't enough wagons or boats—or anything! Both the railroad and the canal by which these hospital cases might be brought back here are closed. *Why?* And why is there always this neglect, this shortage of proper rations?"

The Senator, a conscientious man, protested truly that his committee had not been aware of the conditions at Belle Plain.

"Inform your committee!"

"I will, Miss Barton."

He went immediately to the War Department and, though it was night, convened a meeting. At ten o'clock he was saying, "One of two things will have to be done, and right away. Either you'll send someone tonight with the power to investigate and correct the abuses of our wounded or the Senate will send someone tomorrow." At two o'clock in the morning, the Quartermaster General himself galloped to the wharf and the tugboat which would speed him to Belle Plain. At ten, he had instituted an investigation. At noon, the abuses had been considerably corrected.

In June of 1864, Clara accepted the appointment of Superintendent of Nurses for the Army of the James, which was then commanded by General Ben Butler. It was an executive position. She had under her many nurses, stewards, orderlies, and clerks; she conferred with surgeons and physicians. But also she was a housekeeper on the grand scale. She wrote to Fannie Childs that her family normally comprised fifteen hundred and was sometimes more numerous. She had to plan for it and to move it as the army moved—which, she said, was not precisely a lark. She was not immune to the tribulations of any housekeeper: She had to settle arguments in the kitchen; if the chefs were ill or sulky, she must substitute at the ovens and stoves.

She told Fannie of a typical menu: For breakfast, "seven hundred loaves of bread, one hundred and seventy gallons of hot coffee, two large wash-boilers full of tea, one barrel of apple sauce, one barrel of sliced boiled pork, or thirty hams, one half barrel of cornstarch blanc mange, five hundred slices of butter toast, one hundred slices of broiled steak, and one hundred and fifty patients to be served with chicken gruel, boiled eggs, etc. For dinner we have over two hundred gallons of soup, or boiled dinner of three barrels of potatoes, two barrels of turnips, two barrels of onions, two barrels of squash, one hundred gallons of minute pudding, one wash-boiler full of whiskey sauce for it, or a large tub of codfish nicely picked, and stirred in a batter to make one hundred and fifty gallons of nice home codfish, and the Yankee soldiers cry when they taste it (I prepared it just the old home way, and so I have everything cooked), and the same toasts and cornstarch as for breakfast. And then for supper two hundred gallons of rice, and twenty gallons of sauce for it, two hundred gallons of tea, toast for a thousand; . . . some days I have made with my own hands ninety apple pies."

Once a desperately homesick fellow asked Clara for custard pie. "Out in Missouri where I come from, we have it yellow and fluffy, ma'am, with crinkly edges."

She nodded. "I know exactly what you mean." As she was fluting the crust, she was reminded of how she had learned this trick with pastry, of the long-ago winter when she and her mother had been shut in together, "getting acquainted."

On another day she baked gingerbread for a group of Wisconsin lads, with her own money purchasing the extra flour and molasses. "If our new milk comes tomorrow," she wrote to Fannie Childs, "we are to commence to make doughnuts. I have a barrel of nice lard ready. . . . Oh, if I could only write you what I have seen, known, heard and done since I first came to this department. The most surprising of all of which is (tell Sally) that I should have *turned cook*. Who would have 'thunk it'?"

Several times daily she went the rounds of the cots, soothing and prescribing. She wrote hundreds of letters for men who wished to inform parents, wives, or sweethearts of their whereabouts. One youth for whom she did this slight service was a Swiss boy named Jules Golay. After that she frequently paused at Jules' bedside, for she liked talking with him.

He had a sincere love for the American ideal. "Your republic is a splendid one, Miss Barton."

"The most splendid in the world. I never question that for an instant, or that it will rise from this ordeal, and from any ordeal it may have to meet in future, as the phoenix rises from ashes. But," Clara said, glancing up and down the aisles of prone and disabled figures, "God's price *is* high."

In September she told Fannie Childs, "I have a *whole* house of my own, first and second floors, two rooms and a flight of stairs, and a great big fireplace, a bright fire burning, with an arbor of cedar in front of it and all around it, so close and green that a cat couldn't look in. . . . It was the Negro house for the plantation, and was dirty, of course, but ten men with brooms and fifty barrels of water made it all right."

Before the month was out she was to think of her ownership of the house as providential. For abruptly and unexpectedly she had need of it.

16

IT WAS a harrowing day and Clara was in the field, for General Butler pressed at the defenses of Richmond. All morning the stretchers had been arriving at the "flying hospital," a tent erected behind the lines. A dozen surgeons were strenuously busy—there should have been twice as many.

Clara was seated on a coil of rope, supporting a wounded man, when the courier dashed up. "Letter for you, Miss Barton!" She scarcely could take it from him. The poor fellow in her arms must be held just so, until a doctor should examine him.

But the envelope was postmarked "Oxford." Clutching it with one hand, she bent and tore at the flap with her teeth. Enclosed was a second envelope. From Norfolk, Virginia? But who was writing to her from there? She read both letters—incredulously—and looked back into the tent. The doctor? Where was he? She must wait for him, though she wanted nothing so much as to drop her burden—and run!

At last the doctor appeared. "This man has been shot through the lungs," she said, and got to her feet. Yet even then she must stop, to wash her stained hands. It seemed hours before she could hurry to an empty ambulance, jump into it and hurtle off along the road to General Butler's headquarters.

He was engrossed with his maps and charts, counseling with his officers, but she pushed in. And, as always, he greeted her with profound respect.

148

"General, I have heard from my brother Stephen."

"Really, Miss Barton! Where is he?"

"In Norfolk. A prisoner. He has been very ill, and thought finally that he must venture from his home for medicine. He started in a light farm wagon, with some clothing and three thousand dollars in cash in his wallet. But he was too ill to go far. He became unconscious. A raiding party found him—it was your raiding party, General Butler, our own men! I suppose the money made them suspicious. Anyway, they charged Stephen with being a vagrant, a thief, and hustled him off to Norfolk and threw him into a house crowded with criminals and with the plague-stricken. And there he's been for six weeks. He has no idea that I'm so near him. He wrote to our relatives in Oxford. He bribed a Negro urchin to mail the letter for him—my nephew forwarded it to me."

The general frowned. "This is hard for you, Miss Barton. What can I do?"

"Stephen is blameless—"

"Yes, yes, I know. And raiders can be utter fools."

"Let me go to him, General."

"Why not have him come here? Or have you shelter for him?"

"Yes, I have! An old slave cabin on the plantation."

"Then I shall dictate a dispatch to the officer at Norfolk. And since you are so perturbed, Miss Barton, why not retire to your cabin and get it in shape for the invalid? As soon as he arrives, I'll send him to you."

The next two days and nights seemed endless. Little time was required for Clara's preparations. An orderly built a bunk in the cabin's small loft and stuffed another mattress with straw. She aired blankets, rummaged through her bags for towels and a pillow·slip. And then she had nothing more to do but wait.

Late in the third night, steps sounded outside the cedar arbor. She flung open the door.

"Stephen!"

Two soldiers were there, escorting a pale, stooped man tottering on a cane.

"Hello, Clara." His voice was husky. He was white-bearded, and his white hair hung to his thin shoulders. But his eyes twinkled. "General Butler just told me you were here. I asked, 'Is my sister a prisoner too?'"

As the soldiers withdrew, she seated him in a chair and knelt beside him. "Dear Stephen!"

"I've changed a good deal, I guess."

"No!" she exclaimed—and thought of him as he had been six years ago when last she saw him, so sturdy and muscular, so strong and bronzed, and of the morning when he had driven her to the station to catch the train for Clinton ("I like my life as it is," he'd said, and, "Luck, Clara!"), and of a thousand and one other mornings, each with its memories. Stephen, the big brother on whom she leaned, who loved and was proud of her. "Yes," she said, "you've changed, and so have I. Yet some things never change—and we are still wonderfully the same."

Stephen would be a long time rallying from the shock of his capture and imprisonment. Meanwhile, there was no better refuge for him than here, where Clara could care for him. All winter he occupied the cabin. Every minute to be spared from the hospital and field work she spent with him.

He slept badly. Often she sat up all night, talking to him, diverting him from pain and worries. They discussed family matters, and the war and politics. Sherman was marching from Atlanta to the sea; in February he reclaimed Charleston. Sheridan, Thomas, Butler, and the other commanders were pulling the net tighter about a strangling but defiant Confederacy. Grant was hammering at Richmond. Lee's army had been taxed by desertions and by the bickering among the governments of the several Southern states. Lee was a peerless leader, but sorely beset by fate and eventualities. President Lincoln had been re-elected.

The fires burned low before Richmond and along the Appomattox and the James. Sentinels picketed, and in the soft spring dusk, men's melancholy voices echoed:

> "We're tenting tonight on the old camp ground,
> Give us a song to cheer
> Our weary hearts, a song of home
> And friends we love so dear;
> Tenting tonight, tenting tonight,
> Tenti on the old camp ground."

On March 4, 1865, Abraham Lincoln at his second inaugural eloquently repeated his pledge of faith to the cause to which he was dedicated:

"With malice toward none; with charity for all; with firmness in the right, as God gives us to see the right, let us strive on to finish the work we are in; to bind up the nation's wounds . . . to do all which may achieve and cherish a just and lasting peace among ourselves and with all nations."

Clara had been resting briefly in the darkness of the cabin loft. The rattle of musketry was almost intolerable, yet through it she caught Stephen's muttering as he lay in his bunk downstairs. What was he saying? She crept down the ladder and stood in the shadows. She could see him, hunched upon hands and knees under the blanket, his face partly buried in the pillow.

"O God, whose children we all are, look down with thine eyes of justice and mercy upon this terrible conflict. . . . O God, save my country. Bless Abraham and his armies!"

He paused, raised his head. "Clara?"

"Yes, it's I."

"What is that dreadful noise? No, don't tell me. I know. Grant is storming Richmond, his cannon pounding incessantly."

She went and clasped his hand in hers.

"Pray with me, Clara. . . . O our God, stay this strife. Proclaim through the sacrifices of the people, a people's freedom, and through the sufferings of a nation, a nation's peace."

So they prayed, while around them the last guns of the war thundered and destroyed.

On April 3, 1865, Richmond surrendered.

The Confederacy had collapsed; the Union had been preserved.

Part Three

17

T HE cannon of Appomattox scarcely had cooled before Clara was in Washington and there launching upon a new enterprise. "If I were to speak of war," she once said, "it would not be to show you the glories of conquering armies, but the mischief and misery they strew in their track." Perhaps some of the mischief and the misery could be counteracted. She thought so.

She went to the White House to see Abraham Lincoln, and even in the midst of pressing affairs of state, he received her. This little woman had done much for her country; she was privileged beyond ordinary folk.

"Mr. President," Clara said, "I want to conduct a search for our unreported soldiers. There are thousands of them—in unmarked graves, in prison camps, or listed simply as missing. Those imprisoned will ultimately be released; the missing may be only wandering somewhere, temporarily or permanently lost, or they might be fugitives. I feel, though, that too many have been classed as deserters and a false stigma set against their names. It is my honest belief that our army records show a larger number of deserters than we ever really had. Probably no one is to blame for this. The very nature of the area over which we fought, the wildness of the territory, and the duration of time—all these circumstances conspired against the keeping of any accurate record. Yet it would be most unfair if a single patriot were branded with a disgrace he did not rate."

She paused and looked up at the President. He had altered in appearance, she thought. The war years had taken tremendous toll of him, grooving his face with deep furrows, grizzling his hair and beard. But nothing could dim the steady kindliness of his eyes, the tenderness and humor of his fine mouth, the greatness and humility of his manner.

"Go on, Miss Barton," he said.

She told him then what was behind her suggestion: how she had undergone long anxiety in that period when her brother Stephen had been beyond reach. And there had been Hugh Johnson at Chantilly, and Donald, the young Confederate, in the Lacy House at Fredericksburg, who had said that "uncertainty can be crueler than out-and-out bad news," and the scores of men in the Virginia hospitals for whom she had written letters.

"The thing they yearned for most, Mr. President, was to be in touch with home and loved ones. They worried for their families rather than for themselves. They wanted their parents, their wives or sweethearts to know what had become of them. Recently, too, I have read some of the newspaper lists of the missing—which, to some minds, means the *deserters*. In just a random glance I found three names which I know didn't belong there. Charley Hamilton: he was shot at Bull Run; I held him in my arms when he died. He had been a pupil in my school at Bordentown. I remember how he used to wait for me outside the school door and carry my satchel. I cannot bear for Charley Hamilton to be reported as a deserter! And Mr. Greene: he was the sexton of our church in North Oxford. I was with the orderlies who picked him up on the shore of the Rappahannock. I tended him and got him onto the train, bound for Georgetown. I believed he had recovered. I know Mr. Greene was not faithless to his duty! And Sergeant Thomas Farley of Indiana: he is another of those listed as missing. I met Sergeant Farley only once, but I am indebted to him. It is quite inconceivable that such a man should have hidden away or shown the white feather. I know that Thomas Farley had no close relatives, but I want to find him—or, if I can't, I want to learn truly what happened to him. I want to clear his name!"

She paused again, and Mr. Lincoln nodded.

"Mr. President, we need a bureau to straighten out these things. I have thought about it a good deal. If I had needed more incentive, I've found it in the entreaties of civilians. The country seems to know that I had an agency for the distribution of supplies and that, in so doing, I traveled near and far—"

"Yes, Miss Barton." The President smiled. "The country knows that pretty well."

"Now people are asking me to be an agent to distribute information. I am willing to try. But I must be businesslike and thorough about it. And, if possible, I must have government backing. That's why I've come to you."

"And you shall have government backing, Miss Barton." He laid his big, sinewy hand sympathetically on her shoulder. "You shall have your headquarters at Annapolis. That's the depot for exchange of prisoners from Southern camps. Will you call upon General Hitchcock? He is the commandant at Annapolis. I think he will co-operate with you."

Clara noted in her journal that she had "a most delightful interview" with General Hitchcock. He said that the establishment of such a bureau would not be easy, but she would be sustained. "He would stand between me and all harm," Clara wrote. "He felt no person in the United States would oppose me. . . . The President was there too."

General Hitchcock said that as a preliminary he would have new and comprehensive lists of all unreported soldiers printed and posted conspicuously in every town and village. Correspondence would be invited from anyone who could furnish information. Clara would have a staff of clerks, paid for by the government.

Within the week she was ready to begin, heralded by the impressive title of "General Correspondent for the Friends of Paroled Prisoners." Letters were pouring in, literally bushels of them, stacked into huge baskets. More letters arrived with each mail. Soon the bureau would be flourishing. And then on April 14, everything stopped.

For on that day, the blackest in American history, Abraham Lincoln was assassinated.

The impact of the tragedy was staggering. Hearts cried out in grief. In his immortal hymn, Walt Whitman, America's "good, gray poet," sang the sorrow of a whole people:

"When lilacs last in the door-yard bloom'd,
  And the great star early droop'd in the western sky in the
    night,
  I mourn'd, and yet shall mourn with ever-returning spring."

For a while Clara floundered in a quandary. Yet even as she wept for Abraham Lincoln, she thought she must go on with an endeavor which he had endorsed. He had seen the bureau as a solace to those who had sacrificed husbands, brothers, sons. Perhaps to abandon it now would be a breach of trust. She made haste to speak with Andrew Johnson and discovered that he was of the same opinion. That sincere and often misunderstood statesman had come to the Presidency in a moment of climax, but to the best of his ability he would perpetuate the Emancipator's ideals.

"I know what Mr. Lincoln thought of your quest, Miss Barton," Andrew Johnson said. "And I concur in his view of it. You must proceed."

By the time summer had rolled around, Clara had organized her bevy of clerks and devised methods of handling her immense mail. She could announce results. More than a thousand of the men she sought had been located—and, of course, they were not traitors at all, but honorable men who rejoiced at being reinstated in the good graces of the world and of their various communities. The families of another thousand had been told when and where their heroes had fallen in battle.

One day Clara had an almost illegible letter from a town in eastern Maryland:

Der Mis Barton, this is to infom you Mr. Farley, sargent from Indianny he is still aliving.

Much excited, Clara deciphered the badly spelled and jumbled sentences. The writer was a widowed woman, who, with her son, tilled a few scrawny hillside acres. On a dark night, after Spotsylvania, a wounded man had stumbled into her cabin. He was half blind, delirious. The woman had nursed him back to consciousness, and he was "still aliving."

Sergeant Thomas Farley? Clara knew what to do. She communicated with a girl in "Indianny." And she was very happy. It was moments like this which made the work worthwhile.

But, as General Hitchcock had said, the management of the bureau was not easy. Soon the funds allotted for its maintenance ran low. Clara unhesitatingly drew upon her personal funds and hired additional clerks and forged indomitably ahead. And there were times when she felt that she was not getting results as fast or in the volume which she wished. A thousand, two thousands, a friend located here and there—that was only a drop in the bucket! She wanted to do much more. Many inquiries came to her which she could not answer. And what about the Southern prisons? What information had she collected about Andersonville, for instance? Northern soldiers by the hundreds had been committeed to Andersonville and there had vanished as completely as though the earth opened and swallowed them. Prisoners were being exchanged at Annapolis, were being restored to their homes. But none from Andersonville. Why? Where were the men from this most infamous of Southern stockades?

And Clara Barton did not know. Until the day when an emaciated youth in a faded uniform limped into her office.

He was Dorrence Atwater and just out of the hospital.

"I read of you in the newspaper, Miss Barton," he said. "I have a story which might interest you."

It was a curious story. At sixteen Dorrence Atwater had enlisted in a squadron of Connecticut cavalry. Captured in 1863, he had been taken to Georgia, to Andersonville. He was very ill there, for filth and squalor and disease were rampant, hunger stalked, and men slept naked in the swamps or burrowed into the earth like moles.

"My comrades were dying all around me. Dying like flies. I thought I'd die, too. To this minute I can't see why I didn't. Somehow, though, I shook off the fever—enough, at least, to be set to keeping the daily death roll in the surgeon's tent."

He was nineteen then, but older in judgment than in years, for he had the wit to know that this record he was making was valuable—and also that it might never be revealed. He was listing a hundred deaths each day, most of them caused by starvation or brutal mistreatment.

"I figured that whether or not the South won the war—and it looked like they would—no prison authorities ever could afford to have the facts brought to light about what happened down there. The roll of the burials, the names, the men's regiment numbers, the places within the stockade where the bodies were planted in coffinless graves—I thought all that never would be known, unless—unless I kept a duplicate record."

Dorrence Atwater sighed. "But suppose I never left, myself. I thought of that, Miss Barton. Plenty of ghastly mornings when I couldn't see how I'd last through the day. Well, maybe I could smuggle the duplicate to some friend. Anyway, I decided to try."

He had to be stealthy. Everything was so hazardous, even the securing of extra sheets of paper. He must evade the guards' eyes. But, having started, he persevered. When, in a trade, he was bundled off to Salisbury prison and then, at length, to Annapolis, he carried the duplicate roll sewed into the lining of his tunic.

"And here it is." He took a sheaf of soiled papers from some inner pocket, tossed them on Clara's desk. "I guess you're the one to have it now."

Breathlessly Clara studied the pages. Here it was, the tale of Andersonville's degradation, the facts about what happened there.

"You were quite right," she said, "in thinking that the original would be destroyed. There's no estimating how many people have been wanting a disclosure, and despairing of ever getting one. This diagram you've drawn, could you interpret it? If you went to Andersonville, could you point out the individual graves?"

Dorrence Atwater smiled ruefully. "I know every inch of that stockade, the sand stretches, the caves, the tunnels, and the forts, the dungeons with their balls and chains, the sentry stalls and the kennels for bloodhounds. I couldn't forget it, Miss Barton. But I'm not going down there."

"We'll see," Clara said. "We'll see."

18

"You have done some quite remarkable things in the past, Miss Barton," said Secretary of War Stanton, "and always without the assistance of my department, though I should have been glad to give it. What, specifically, are you asking now?"

"Transportation for myself and Dorrence Atwater and a detachment of laborers, who will build a proper fence around the burial lot and mark each grave with a suitable headboard."

Mr. Stanton seemed to muse. "You are a clever person—"

"No, I'm not."

"No? They say you've never yet miscalled an army officer, never mistaken a colonel for a major." He grinned teasingly. "I think that's being clever."

"My father was a soldier, Mr. Secretary. He taught me military etiquette."

"Which you haven't forgotten, eh? Well, you wouldn't propose the unraveling of this Andersonville confusion if it weren't practical, I daresay. But it will be morbid and grueling work in the midsummer heat. And for a lady—"

"Yes, I'm a lady. And probably I'm a sentimentalist, too," Clara said. "Anyway, I'm concerned for thirteen thousand families scattered over the North and the West. I'm thinking of their feeling of satisfaction when they hear that their soldier dead have had Christian interment under headboards which bear their own names."

"That may be sentimentalism, Miss Barton. It's also common sense. How many laborers will you require? I'll send Captain Moore to supervise them."

They went by boat from Washington to Savannah and journeyed inland to Andersonville. On July 26, Clara wrote to Secretary Stanton that no serious obstacles had been encountered, the graves were being rapidly marked.

". . . We can accomplish fully all that we came to accomplish, and the field is wide and ample for much more in the future. If *desirable,* the grounds of Andersonville can be made a National Cemetery of great beauty and interest. Be assured, Mr. Stanton, that for this prompt and humane action of yours, the American people will bless you long after your willing hands and mind have ceased to toil for them."

Morbid and grueling work, the Secretary of War had said. But there were compensations in it, and on the day when she saw the cemetery enclosed and protected, she felt that she was well rewarded. A tall and shining metal flagpole stood at the gate of the twenty-five acres which had been the stockade. It was Clara Barton's solemn honor to raise the United States flag for the first time since their death above these silent men who had died to preserve it.

Back again at Annapolis, she planned for the publication of the Andersonville roll. She had friends in the journalistic world. Among them she chose to consult Horace Greeley, the distinguished editor of the *New York Tribune.*

Mr. Greeley told her what she herself had surmised, that the list was too extensive for printing in the columns of any newspaper. He advised her to compile the thirteen thousand names into a booklet, and this she did. February 14, 1866, was the date fixed for the issuing of the booklet. That day Horace

Greeley ran throughout the edition of the *Tribune,* in several places on every page the one word "Andersonville," in heavy black type, and in other places a line of capitals, "Andersonville; See advertisement on 8th page." No one who read the newspaper could have escaped knowing that the much-talked-of roll was ready for publication. Also the *Tribune* contained an article by Clara Barton, in which she told all about the identifying of the thirteen thousand graves.

Booklet and article were hailed with nationwide eagerness and brought comfort to many saddened homes.

The search for missing men expanded steadily after that. As a consequence, perhaps, Clara had offers of lecture engagements. Her first impulse was to say no, emphatically. She was so shy of people. She could speak to a schoolroom or to a regiment. But as for making a speech before an audience— why, she'd never thought of such a thing!

Yet, as she reviewed them, the offers took on a certain significance. She was really rather hard-up, financially. What part of her Patent Office salary which hadn't gone to paying for a substitute clerk had been lavished on her storeroom. And with the launching of the Annapolis bureau, this salary had been cut off. She was earning nothing here. Moreover, she had so frequently dipped into her savings and the sum which had come to her as an inheritance from her father's estate that her bank account was reduced to a minimum. Money in itself mattered very little to her, but certainly she had no intention of becoming dependent upon charity. And maybe lecturing would further the success of the bureau. Clubs and societies were wanting to hear, directly from her, about her wartime experiences. ("Just a plain recital, Miss Barton," they told her. "You can give that.") At last she consented, visualizing the interest she might create and how stimulating the publicity would be to her work.

She went first to Worcester—"a dress rehearsal," she said, "for the home folks"—and then to Oxford. This, she jotted in her diary, was "the pleasantest lecture I shall ever deliver." From there she went to neighboring cities. Her audiences were everywhere most enthusiastic. Of course she had stage fright (she had expected that), but she subdued it.

As the demand increased, Clara had to make more and longer tours, through New England, the Middle West, across the Mississippi into the West. Usually she was alone, but sometimes Dorrence Atwater accompanied her, for people were clamoring to hear the story of his Andersonville adventures.

Clara carefully noted in her diary each of her lecture engagements, and she kept a scrapbook of press clippings which were invariably complimentary, describing her speeches as "thrilling" and "inspiring," and herself as "small and charming, modestly attired in black silk; with a clear, ringing voice which transports her listeners to the scenes she so vividly pictures." Often in the throngs would be war veterans whom she had nursed, or doctors who had known her in Virginia or at Hilton Head. On such occasions, informal reunions would be held after the lecture, or perhaps the old friend would rise and add his reminiscences to Clara's.

The tours were profitable, both to Clara and to her bureau. She might have protracted them for several years, but for their physical drain upon her.

The end came dramatically—as did so many of the incidents in Clara Barton's existence. One winter evening in 1868, she stood on the platform of an Eastern city's opera house, confronting a pit and galleries entirely filled. She was speaking, midway through her lecture. She was telling about Falmouth, the Lacy House—

Suddenly she could not utter another word. Her throat seemed paralyzed. Her "clear, ringing voice" had gone. Mutely she gazed out over the waiting theater, the faces of women fashionable in jewels and furs, of men with gleaming white collars above broadcloth coats. How quiet they were, so polite! Waiting.

She smiled, tried again to say something—anything. Then she shook her head and walked slowly from the stage.

The lecturing was over. The doctor diagnosed her ailment as a return of the nervousness she had had in Bordentown.

"Your throat is exhausted, as it was then. Rest is the cure. Why don't you go abroad?"

"I can rest at home," she whispered.

"But would you? I think not, Miss Barton," the doctor said. "No, you ought to go to Europe and stay for three years."

"*Three years?*"

"That's my order. As the best of American troopers, you won't disobey it, Miss Barton."

So, in September 1869, she sailed for Europe.

19

THE voyage was refreshing. Reclining for hours in a deck chair under a cloudless sky, Clara reflected that illness, if she must endure it, had descended upon her at a proper time. She had money—the fees from lectures and also the sum of fifteen thousand dollars granted by a recent Act of Congress to reimburse her for her personal expenditures in the bureau—all of which she had invested rather shrewdly. With her simple tastes, she could live on the income from these investments. And the work of the bureau had tapered to a logical conclusion: she had done everything that could be done in the search for the missing, otherwise she would not have forsaken it.

Now she could relax and be once more like her younger self, the little girl who pored over Menseur's *Geography,* to whom the prospect of blue ocean and foreign lands was alluring.

She disembarked in Scotland and went from there to London, then to Paris and then to Switzerland, to Geneva where the climate was said to be favorable to throat afflictions. She had friends in this city: the Golays, the family of the Swiss boy for whom she had written letters in General Butler's base hospital in Virginia. Jules' mother and his sister were grateful to Clara Barton and never had lost sight of her. Now they wished to entertain her.

Perhaps, too, inscrutable destiny turned Clara toward Geneva —though she did not suspect it.

The Golays were charming and hospitable folk. They made their guest welcome and at ease. Their neighbors called upon her. But one morning ten dignified gentlemen who were strangers to the Golays and to Clara alike came calling. Bearded, silk-hatted, frock-coated, they were a committee from the International Convention of Geneva, with Dr. Louis Appia as leader and spokesman.

"We are here, Miss Barton," Dr. Appia announced, after an interval of ceremonious bowing, "to inquire of you, the most illustrious of American women, why the United States has refused to sign the treaty of Geneva, which provides for the relief of sick and wounded soldiers. Your country's position is incomprehensible to us. If the treaty had originated in some monarchical government, we might credit the refusal. On the contrary, it originated in Switzerland, which is a republic older than your own. To what does America object? How can these objections be overcome? Will you not explain, madam?"

Dumfounded, Clara stared at Dr. Appia. She had no notion whatever of either the Convention or the treaty.

"Twice," continued Dr. Appia, "and formally, your government at Washington has been approached. In both instances we were rebuffed. This has amazed us." He stroked his luxuriant beard. "We had thought Americans were a humane people."

"They are," Clara asserted quickly. "The most humane people in the world."

"We had supposed their hearts would warm to a policy which would save lives, prevent cruelty—"

"They would! No one knows so well as I how warm are American hearts."

"Then why—"

Clara frowned. "Dr. Appia, I am quite in the dark on this topic. I have been for years immersed in just such an enterprise as you mention, the saving of lives, the prevention of cruelty. Most of that time I was striving as an individual—and succeeding only because the innate kindliness of my countrymen sustained me in my efforts. If your convention is fair and good and effective, I am sure that America would wish to join it, and does not know she has refused. We have just been through a dreadful war, the more dreadful that it was between Americans, brother against brother. While it was in progress, Congress could consider no business except that connected with the war. Your treaty has never been submitted to the American people—of that I'm positive, or I should have heard of it."

"We have mailed much literature," Dr. Appia said.

"Printed in French?"

"And in German, yes."

"But we are an English-speaking people. Your literature could not have been widely read."

"You are a French student, Miss Barton?"

"To an extent, I am."

"Then," Dr. Appia said, nodding to the other gentlemen, "we shall leave with you this pamphlet, *Un Souvenir de Solferino,* which we respectfully ask you to study. And we shall interview you later, if we may, Miss Barton, at your convenience, to learn your opinions." He rose and bowed. All the frock coats bowed. "We devoutly hope for your sanction and your help. We all know of your great ability. No American citizen is more distinguished or beloved."

Clara took the little book into the Golays' rear garden, where the air was clear and bracing, autumn flowers colored the brick wall, and Mont Blanc loomed, snow-capped, in the distance, and there she read attentively *Un Souvenir de Solferino.*

The author, one Henri Dunant, a Swiss, had happened to be in northern Italy following the battle of Solferino, at which the Austrians were defeated by the allied armies of Italy and France. The medical corps of an army was then without any treaty protection and must trail in the wake of its own troops, whether pursuing or pursued. As an eyewitness, Monsieur Dunant saw the wounded trampled underfoot, often abandoned. He encountered them, languishing, neglected, dying, in villages near the battlefront. And so appalled was he that he recruited a body of volunteers whose purpose was to mitigate the pains of all sufferers, Italians, French, and Austrian, observing no dividing lines of nationality. His pamphlet, written in 1862, was a recounting of Monsieur Dunant's experiment. In it he put the question:

"Would it not be possible to found and organize in all civilized countries permanent societies of volunteers which in time of war would render succor to the wounded *without distinction of nationality?"*

Translated into various languages, *Un Souvenir de Solferino* had challenged not only the peoples, but also the rulers of Europe. In Monsieur Dunant's native Geneva, the Société Génévoise d'Utilité Publique already existed to promote the very causes which he was urging. This organization brought together at Geneva in October 1863 representatives of fourteen nations to draft an agreement designed to attain "the relief of the wounded in armies at the field." In August 1864 a second convention was held, to which twenty-five sovereign states were invited, and sixteen responded by sending delegates. Here by vote an international pact was adopted "to render neutral and immune from injury in war the sick and wounded and all who cared for them."

Since 1864, the Convention had met regularly, perfecting its organization. Its emblem was a red cross on a white ground, a reversal of the white cross on red ground of the Swiss national banner and chosen as a tribute to the government of Switzerland, which had so steadfastly advanced the Convention's ideals.

"There is something in this," mused Clara Barton, as she finished reading Monsieur Dunant's treatise. "A great deal. It's what I've thought of, what I talked about to David. Not the haphazard generosity of impulsive civilians—but order and system. I've dreamed of that."

She remembered the mild criticism of Dr. Appia and his gentlemen for an America which would not become officially a part of the Geneva Convention. At that meeting held in August 1864, two Americans had been seated. They were the United States Minister to Switzerland, Mr. George C. Fogg, and the European agent of the United States Sanitary Commission, Mr. Charles S. P. Bowles. But they had been cautioned to attend *"in an informal manner"* only, and to confine their participation merely to the giving and taking of suggestions— and there the interest of America in an international compact had ended.

"That was natural," Clara thought. "In 1864, we could not see beyond our own catastrophe. We had to get the Civil War behind us; we had our internal readjustments to make. If, as Dr. Appia says, the treaty was presented afterward to the United States Government, it must have been sidetracked in some bureau. The people have not rejected it, and wouldn't. Three years from now, when I am at home again, I shall plead for it."

What she did not know was that an attempt previously had been made to arouse the American public in behalf of the International Red Cross. At the close of the Civil War, Dr. Henry W. Bellows, president of the United States Sanitary Commission, had proposed the founding of "The American Association for the Relief of Misery of Battlefields" and had spoken with great frankness of the inadequacy of even such splendid bodies as the Sanitary Commission, which he headed. "Good intentions and humane sentiments are not alone qualified for this duty," Dr. Bellows said, and begged for the extending and universalizing of mercy toward the victims of war.

Dr. Bellows failed utterly—"ignominiously," as he later asserted. The United States Government had little time just then for philanthropies which reached outside its own borders, nor did it feel very kindly toward European monarchies for their attitude in regard to the American Civil War. Dr. Bellows acknowledged himself as thoroughly discouraged and tried no more.

Clara Barton, meditating in the Golays' garden, knew none of this. Yet, even had she been aware of the situation, her conviction that *she* must do something would probably have been the same.

Shunning the cold of mountain weather, Clara spent the winter in Corsica. Then she returned to Switzerland, paused at Geneva and, vexed that her throat should still be so delicate, went on to the mineral baths at Bern. Somewhat improved, she was in Bern, staying with the American consul and his wife, in July 1870 when all Europe was electrified by Napoleon's declaration of war upon the kingdom of Prussia.

In a letter to David, Clara depicted the suspense of Switzerland as it viewed the menace of mobilizing troops. That was in the haying season. The country was very beautiful.

"It is the custom to cut all the grass fields twice and the first cutting is being done now, the field just in front of my windows is being mowed today. The cows are out on the sides of the mountains with the dairymen and women and the shepherds. There must be a lot of fruit by the promise of the trees. The peaks of the Bernese Alps, always white with snow, are in plain sight—when there is not an Indian summer haze over everything. . . . Today France and Prussia with both Northern and Southern Germany are armed and marching to the Rhine, and little Switzerland, bright as a diamond in her rough setting, proclaiming a neutrality which she means. Through all her valleys come her sturdy, brown-cheeked mountain farmers in their neat uniforms of blue, with knapsack and cartridge-box, forty thousand troops to line her borders and preserve her liberty at any cost."

No one could believe in war as a reality, Clara said. "Even the Prussian press said it 'could not be,' it was *zu dumm*. But the reader of history has yet to learn that nothing can be 'too foolish,' and no pretext too slight, where personal interest, royal ambition or pride are threatened. 'To the Rhine!' rings out on every side. *'Vive la guerre!'* "

Perhaps it was that same sunny afternoon, and Clara had just laid down her pen, when the procession rumbled to the portals of the American consulate. Outriders were ahead, resplendent in the flashing gold and scarlet liveries of the royal house of Baden. After them rolled a coach, rich with trappings. As the horses halted, a footman leaped down and knocked on the consul's door; with a white gloved hand he gave a card to the consul's butler. Then the footman opened the coach door and a lady alighted.

Young and pretty, fashionably attired, she was the Grand

Duchess of Baden, the daughter of King William of Prussia. She had been in the Alps, at one of her castles, but Napoleon's declaration had called her home.

"I have come these miles out of my way to see you, Miss Barton. I am a subscriber to the work of the Geneva Convention. I believe in it with all my soul. Now my country is to be involved in what will doubtless be a bitter war. Will you not aid us?"

Clara had conversed with presidents and generals and ambassadors, but never before with a grand duchess, yet she was too much the Yankee to be awed.

"I am an American," she said. "A private citizen."

"And a nurse."

"Yes, I have been that, and a sort of impromptu and amateur sanitary commissioner—"

"Be one of us, Miss Barton!" begged the grand duchess. "We are swayed by those very emotions which dominate your heart. Our Red Cross society is so new. It has material resources but a dearth of skilled directors, whereas your name is the synonym for efficiency. You have the habit of *getting things done.*"

"I am in Bern to recuperate."

"And are you not better, Miss Barton? But do not feel that you must reply to this petition immediately. Only say that you will think about it!"

Clara was thinking about it (indeed, she'd thought of nothing else!) when, a week later, Dr. Appia with Monsieur Gustave Moynier, president of the Geneva Convention, and other officials passed through the city en route to Basel, which would be the Red Cross focal point. Again Dr. Appia spoke to Miss Barton: She understood the theory of the Red Cross now— would she not like to watch that theory translated into practice? Would she not lend herself to the emergency?

"It's strange, my being here at all," said Clara. "Almost as if foreordained. But many of the occurrences of my life have been like that. Yes, I'll follow you gentlemen to Basel."

The American consul and his wife protested. What of her throat, her voice? This was sheer idiocy and they would not permit it!

"But," Clara said, "as the Grand Duchess Louise reminded me, I am so much better. Let me go."

Basel was just at the German border. The town would surely be in the path of King William's invasion of France. Its population was in a furor of apprehension. Yet at the Red Cross headquarters calm prevailed, and the atmosphere of industry, for this was the property which the armies of both Germany and France had guaranteed protection. No cannon would be leveled upon it. Since the warehouses flew the Red Cross flag, they would be unmolested.

These warehouses Clara inspected. The stock there was much larger than any ever assembled by the United States Sanitary Commission, and every train brought into Basel barrels and crates to augment it—and also numbers of trained nurses, each with the Red Cross badge on breast or armband.

How different was this from the chaos Clara had witnessed at home. But, she sighed, if only none of it were necessary, if only peace could be kept. And, except for the greed and stupidity of men in high place, it could be. And why should one half the race be in duty bound to tie up the hurts, repair the damage, inflicted by the other half?

She had, alas, no answer.

When she had been several days in Basel, Clara was told to go on to Mulhouse, in France, and she was introduced to a

Swiss girl, Antoinette Margot, who would be her companion. Miss Margot, young and blonde and blue-eyed, had been an art student. Now she was volunteering for Red Cross work.

"It will be my honor to show you the way to Mulhouse, Miss Barton. That is," said Miss Margot, smiling, "if you will have me. I have secured a carriage."

It would be a journey of some twenty miles. Clara packed her satchel and donned a mackintosh, for it was raining. Then she was ready to start.

20

Tʜᴀᴛ was no ordinary drive. A mile out from Basel and they were detained by pickets and made to display their credentials. Six miles, and they were contending against a maelstrom of refugees who fled from invasion to Switzerland's neutrality. The handsome vehicles of the prosperous, farmers' wagons, peasants' carts, filled the road; oxen, cows, goats, dogs, chickens; men and women afoot, laden with household treasures; plodding children with tear-stained, puzzled faces—all swept by terror, and crying, "The Prussians are coming!" Sometimes a hand would snatch at the reins of Clara's horses and a voice would shout: "Turn back! You will be killed!" Then she would say, "No, no. We are nurses, on our way to the front." And the hand would drop and the voice exclaim, *"Mon Dieu!*—God bless you!"

At Mulhouse they were given a message from Dr. Appia to go on to Strasbourg. But the railroad had been blown up. Perhaps if they could drive to Schlettstadt, they might there get a train. Clara's driver, once dismissed, had vanished, and much time was consumed in finding another carriage, for the civilians obviously thought this American lady was insane even to desire one. Finally at daybreak they had hired a particularly brave coachman and were again on the road. After twenty-four hours of rain and mud and several transfers of conveyances, they reached Strasbourg, alighted, and trudged up to the walls of that garrisoned city, where they stood under the ramparts and waited until the gigantic gates should swing to admit them.

For Strasbourg was about to be bombarded—and knew it. The march of the German troops had been fast and ruthless. Though the war might be said to be of France's making, the Prussians were prepared for its prosecution in the most minute detail and with Teutonic foresight would fight it on French soil. To seize Paris was their goal—and to spread panic and desolation behind them. The ancient city of Strasbourg was in their line of march.

As luck would have it, both the United States consul and the vice-consul at Strasbourg were veterans of the American Civil War, and both knew Clara Barton. They said she could not possibly remain within the walls, for when the gates had closed at nightfall they would not reopen until the city's fate had been decided. Already many of the inhabitants had fled, though the majority preferred to stay and doggedly face their punishment. The consul had got an omnibus, which would take away all Americans then visiting in Strasbourg and any other aliens who were eager to be out of Alsace.

"Where do you wish to go, Miss Barton?" the consul queried.

"Where I can be of service."

"There's a huge depot for the wounded at Karlsruhe, housed in a castle of the Grand Duchess Louise of Baden."

"That will be as good a place for me as any. Dr. Appia instructed me no farther than Strasbourg, and now he seems to be lost in the shuffle. I had somehow thought," Clara said, "to work behind the French lines, that I should be needed there. But it is not for me to judge the merits of either army. Nor does that matter. A wounded man is simply a wounded man and must be cared for."

"My omnibus," the consul said, "can take you to the German outposts."

"Thank you," Clara said.

The omnibus floated the Stars and Stripes, and for a while this banner carried it past the pickets stationed at every junction and bridge, but soon the picketing was stricter. When one by one the other passengers had been set down at their several destinations, and only Clara and Miss Margot were in the van, their right to travel was disputed.

The American flag? *"Ach, nein!"* The soldier who halted them laughed in derision. Why, he had been in America, in Mexico. He had seen the flag there—and it was never like this one.

Clara turned to Miss Margot. "Have you the Red Cross badge?"

"Oh, no! I am so sorry, Miss Barton."

"Never mind." Abruptly Clara thought of the bow of red ribbon with which her collar was fastened. She hastily twisted it into a cross and pinned it to her sleeve. Leaning out, she flourished it before the sentry.

"Bitte, Fräulein," he said. "Excuse me," and saluted.

As the omnibus lurched, Clara looked down at the decoration. For the first time she wore the Red Cross insignia. It would not be the last time.

Three miles more and they were just outside a German encampment—troops, horses, wagons everywhere, tents pitched and bayonets guarding the entrance. Here the sentry was so addled at the sight of the two women that he ran to fetch an officer who could deal with the situation.

"You speak English, Colonel?" Clara asked.

"Ein wenig, madam. A trifle. No person can pass into this camp—except on one condition."

"And that is—?"

"As a prisoner of war, madam." He scrutinized her coolly.

"You mean, to be confined?"

"No. The prisoner would be free within our lines, but could not pass out again until the war has ended."

"The wounded will be within your lines. Let me in, Colonel."

"But do you understand the condition? Do you accept it?"

"Yes," Clara said, "I do."

Thus, as a prisoner of war, she rode through the barricade of guns. "Never before," she confided to Antoinette Margot, "has such a thing happened to me. It's amusing, really. My brother David will tease me about this!"

At Karlsruhe, Clara was greeted with joy by the grand duchess. Soon these two were affectionate and trusting friends, a bond which was to continue for a lifetime. Though the political future of her father, King William of Prussia, and of her husband, the ruler of the Duchy of Baden, hinged upon the outcome of this war, Louise seemed more solicitous as to its victims than its victories. She had been one of the earliest members of the Red Cross and had contributed great amounts of money. Now she was giving her time, converting her estates into sanitariums, putting all her property at the disposal of Dr. Appia. She had a genuine and selfless love for humanity— all humanity of whatever race or station. Clara Barton said of her, "I have seen a wounded Arab from the French armies stretch out his arms to her in adoration and blessing as she passed his bed."

Clara's association with Antoinette Margot was just as happy. In this sweet and gentle girl she found a delightful companion. With Karlsruhe as a center, Clara went out to the battle-

fields. Occasionally she paused to marvel: she had thought
never to be so engaged again! After Richmond and Appomattox, she had supposed such labor to be ended for her. It
was as an invalid that she had come to Europe—only to be
involved here in the most strenuous physical exertion. Yet
she could not regard it as drudgery, for she loved it. As before,
she thought of the troops in terms of the individual soldier.
Each man, whether German or French, was important to her,
as she believed him to be important in the eyes of God.

And her health had certainly improved, odd as that might
seem. She felt quite well. And she was learning lessons which
would never be forgotten. Now she was witnessing as a fact
a thing that had been only a visioning: the routine of
meticulously ordered relief, of asylums shielded from attack,
of clean and plenteous supplies, of surgeons, chaplains and
nurses secure from capture and exempted from fear of it,
of convoys of the wounded given a fair chance. Surely it should
be so whenever war came.

Very early one morning, after a night-long vigil, she walked
out the door of an Alsatian villa, which, with its semidetached
sheds and outbuildings, had been commandeered by the Red
Cross as a field hospital. The sun was not yet up, the sky still
overcast with gray. In the half-light the autumn tones of trees
and grass and bushes seemed to glow with a sort of secret
richness of their own. Clara stood looking across a sleeping
camp. The world for the moment was silent and somber. She
felt that she was alone in it, her heart charged with a sense
of the beauty and mystery of human existence, the sublimity
of a natural peace which the martial lords of the race so continuously and so implacably desecrated.

She went a few steps and seated herself on a stool under a
chestnut's yellowing boughs. The sky was gradually brighten-

ing with rosy shafts like the spokes of a fan on the horizon. On one side she could see, sloping down and then up, the many tents in series regular as the links of a chain, wide as a coat of mail thrown by some giant antagonist over a pastoral valley. On the other side, in abrupt contrast, were the ivied walls and ells, the chimneys and shingled roof, the garden plot and orchard of the villa.

High up, in a room under the eaves, where daylight had not yet penetrated, a lamp glowed behind a lowered blind. The lamp of some poor, wakeful sufferer. As Clara watched, the shadow of a nurse's arm and hand was silhouetted in the aperture. Then the glow was extinguished, as the nurse put out the lamp and lifted the blind. Above the window a Red Cross flag rustled with a whispering breeze.

It seemed suddenly to Clara that this had been a symbol. The silhouette—together with the banner. When tragedy swept life from its moorings, in this arm would be strength, in this hand solace, under this flag sanctuary.

But had America repudiated them? "Only because it doesn't know," she murmured softly, and swiftly as a mother might excuse the derelictions of a much-loved child. "If I live to return to my country, I will try to make my people understand."

She had said the words without volition. But with their saying something which had been vague and fluid as a dream was crystallized into a purpose. Clara Barton would make her people understand.

She was seated with the grand duchess on a balcony of the ducal castle in Karlsruhe. The heat of the September afternoon was stifling; the women were resting.

A courier whirled along the path, sprinting at top speed.

Beneath the balcony his knees buckled and he lunged to the ground, crying aloud his message:

"The siege of Strasbourg is over. Strasbourg has fallen."

Clara got to her feet. For weeks the predicament of that beleaguered city had been always in her thoughts. What hardships the inhabitants must have known!

"I am going," she said.

"If you wish," said Louise, "you may cross the Rhine with my husband's escort."

The heavy gates of Strasbourg had been pushed ajar to admit the conquering hordes. But at first glance the city seemed empty. Then, presently, the women and children and aged men stole forth from the cellars in which they had hidden. They were hungry, nearly naked, many of them sick or maimed—twenty thousand without food, raiment, or roofs for their heads.

Clara walked among them, through shattered streets and into cottages wrecked by the bombardment.

"They must be rehabilitated," she said to Antoinette Margot.

"The Red Cross will feed them, Miss Barton."

"I have something else in mind. I shall have a shop here."

"A shop! In this awful shambles?"

"A workroom, where all the Strasbourg women and girls can congregate and work together for their common good. They are hopeless now, Antoinette. Charity is not what they require, so much as new faith in themselves and in one another—and in life."

Antoinette looked at the tumbling walls. "Is there an available building?"

"No. But why not that huge flat rock? The grand duchess will give me cloth and needles and thread. I shall write to my friends in Worcester and Boston and tell of the plight of these innocents who never struck a blow, and would not strike one, and yet have been cursed by the war. My Americans will respond—they always do. Meanwhile, I'll invest my own money in this business!"

The grand duchess, forty days later, saw in Strasbourg an incredible spectacle—Clara's shop, moved now into a school hall which she had finally obtained. Ten girls and three old men sat at tables where, endlessly, it seemed, they measured bolts of cotton cloth into lengths which then were handed to twenty women, who pinned the cloth with paper patterns. Waiting about were more than a hundred other women to fold the cut material into parcels.

"They will carry the parcels to their homes," Clara said, "and return tomorrow or the next day with the completed garments. We are making fifteen hundred garments a week: frocks, chemises, aprons, and pantaloons; shirts, vests, blouses —everything. One group is sewing for the babies—we have a lot of babies!—little gowns and bonnets and winter cloaks. The grandmothers are knitting: hoods and mittens and blankets. We meet here each morning and stay until dusk; and gradually we are thinking not of the siege but of Strasbourg's future."

The grand duchess was so pleased that she offered a large sum of money to be divided among the women. But Clara restrained her.

"These people were not beggars as French subjects. They must not become beggars as Germans. Too much generosity or any suggestion of alms would spoil them. They must regain their self-respect as workers and producers."

"But their poverty is so apparent," said the grand duchess. "They're undernourished, mere skeletons!"

"Yes, I know that they haven't enough food as yet. And I'll

tell you what I should like: to have quantities of groceries with which to pay them for their sewing. They always bring the finished garments back to me in baskets. Market baskets. I want to be able to load those baskets with flour and potatoes and beans and dried apples—and maybe a bit of beef."

"It shall be done," promised the grand duchess.

"Now wasn't that the last thing you would have thought of," Clara wrote home to Oxford, "that I should come to Europe and set up dressmaking, and French dressmaking at that? Well, you should have seen the patterns! And didn't I cut them myself? And didn't I direct all the making until I had imparted my wonderful art to others? And you think my garments are fearfully and wonderfully made? Well, I assure you that they were *nice* garments, and prettily cut, and well made and I found them in excellent demand. Everybody wanted them. And never a complaint of the price. . . . It was such a comfort to see my seamstresses week by week grow better clothed, themselves and the children, till by and by a woman and a baby came to look only like a big and little bundle of the same clothing she carried in her basket. And all the working people of the city came to look like walking bundles of the same clothing. To be sure it took away something from the picturesque style of Strasbourg!"

Clara went to Metz, when the siege had reduced that fortress, and there she established the second of her workshops. But in December she was again in Strasbourg.

"It was Christmas Eve, five o'clock, cold as Greenland," she wrote to her sister Sally Vassall. "I had sent my assistants home the day before to enjoy a few days of leisure with their friends. I was at this farthest end of my room. The postman's rap at my door caused me to look up, and through the curtains I could discern a glimmer of myriad of lights like stars. I rose, suddenly remembering the evening and the occasion.

"The walking out revealed a Christmas tree in full blaze all for myself. It had been arranged and left by my good ladies before their departure. It abounded in fruit, flowers, and mosses and some nice little things which their good hearts had dictated for my comfort; and so in the delicate shadows, falling like tracery beneath its branches, I sat down. . . . I could not truly say that my hand did not sometimes brush across my eyes."

21

THE government of Napoleon III had crashed in September 1870 after the battle of Sedan, calamitous to the French. Since that time the world had known that the cause of France was doomed and the Prussians must ultimately take Paris. Yet for four months Paris held out. Then in January the German Empire was proclaimed in Versailles, and ten days later the victorious Prussian legions entered the city.

Clara Barton, as a member of the Red Cross, went to Paris with the Prussian troops.

The first thing which impressed her as she traversed the wretched streets (walking, of course, for there were no horses to ride in Paris—the horses had all been eaten long ago by a famishing populace) was the serious need for clothing. The winter had been the severest in half a century, and as dangerous an enemy to the French as were the Germans. Quickly as she could, Clara made her way to the mayor's office.

"I have forty thousand garments," she said to the mayor. "They are from the women of Strasbourg, who have clothed themselves and their families and now can help the people of Paris."

She had also other stores in abundance, for an American ship from Boston had docked on the coast, and Clara had arranged a channel by which money and supplies could flow into the Red Cross headquarters.

She was still in Paris, relieving the bereft, in March 1871, when the insurrection of the Commune broke out, a civil war which terminated only with the formal conclusion of the Franco-Prussian War by the signing of the Treaty of Frankfurt on May 10. Again France was a republic—and torn, drained, prostrate. "What the state of France must have been without the merciful help of the Red Cross, imagination does not picture," Clara confided to her diary. "I thanked God that there was never anything in America with which this could be compared."

The conflict might cease; the rehabilitation must persist. And Clara Barton, not a prisoner now (as she whimsically reminded herself) and so well known that her name was a household word, was implored to set up her community sewing rooms in a dozen different French towns.

She was several weeks at Lyon and then at Belfort, where the city officials put her in sole authority and Monsieur l'Administrateur tendered her a room in his own fine residence.

"Here she stands," Antoinette Margot wrote to an American correspondent, "from morning till night, smiling and graceful as always, receiving family after family, and endeavoring to learn by herself what are their circumstances, how deeply they have suffered, to express to them her sympathy, and assist them. . . . It is probable that many of these poor people in this land of aristocracies have never listened to words so respectfully spoken, and are often so overcome by this added kindness of manner extended to them that the first answer which comes is a sob. They are the relics of eight months' siege; the larger portion have lost all or nearly all they possessed, and are homeless, old, broken, dispirited, sick. . . . I only wish, as I always do, that her own people could see their countrywoman at work among the European poor, as not one European has done. If they are proud of her for what she has done at home, they would be prouder of her in a tenfold degree for what she is doing abroad."

The queue outside Monsieur l'Administrateur's door daily averaged two hundred persons, with two policemen to keep the throng in hand. Even so, there were frequent disturbances —when Clara would have to hurry to rescue the policemen from a miniature riot. Her patience was infinite, her good humor proverbial. Her problems were many. To each she gave a separate and thoughtful consideration.

A ragged boy, an old man, a thin woman ("Have you children, madame?" . . . "*Have* I? Dear God, if I have not! Ten children."), a village priest in rusty cassock; an ancient couple, husband and wife, wrinkled and gnarled by fifty years of toil; three little girls, hand in hand, orphaned urchins; a deputation of Catholic Sisters of Mercy in white hats like winged seagulls—so they came to her.

She was spending the funds raised in Boston—this fact she emphasized. The gifts were not from her, but from an American city. Did they comprehend? "*Mais oui! Certainement.* Boston. America. Barton." It was a singsong chant. "Boston-America-*Barton*," the three names forever united in their consciousness.

It was in such surroundings that Antoinette, the erstwhile artist, painted Clara, catching her in characteristic, unposed attitude. The canvas portrays her, small and slender, her head turned toward a baby held by the French peasant woman before her; other women lean forward to hear what Ma'm'selle Barton is saying; children are clinging to her dress: one little waif has lifted a corner of her skirt to his lips.

In November, Clara was invited to Karlsruhe by the grand duchess ("who," as Clara noted in a letter to Sally, "is now Her Imperial Highness since her old papa is no longer King but Emperor") to attend the convening of the Chambers ("— or Parliament or Congress or whatever an English-speaking person would call it," Clara said).

Exactly in contrast with her recent experiences, this one was brilliant and colorful, with tolling bells, rousing cheers, a parade through avenues garlanded with bunting. The Baden dignitaries wore elegant uniforms, frothing with gold lace and plumed helmets. The grand duchess and her pink-cheeked sons and daughters wore blue and white silk. The grand duke was the very figure of benevolent majesty, bowing, seating himself on his crimson throne, rising to read his speech.

"Then," wrote Clara, "all the members one at a time raised the right hand and said '*Ich schwäre,*' which seemed unpardonably wicked of them to swear so *much,* and then it was finished and we came home."

The grand duchess would not allow her friendship with Clara to lapse. She often had her to tea or dinner at the castle, where Clara subsequently met all the royal family of Baden and the grand duchess' mother, the Empress of Germany. Louise was interested in the United States, where she never had visited, and she questioned Clara as to institutions and customs.

"Do you believe," she said one evening, "in the wisdom of educating girls of all classes?"

Clara smiled. "You forget that in my country we have no 'classes.' There we are all alike and none, theoretically at least, is privileged beyond the rest. But I know what you mean. Yes, I do most certainly believe in universal public education, of girls as well as of boys. I believe in woman suffrage, too, and that soon women will have equal political rights with men."

"And you favor a specialized training for the young of both sexes?"

"To a point, yes. But," Clara said, "I think it is possible to drill and discipline too much, until the original vitality has been crushed out and ashes left in place of coals. And if you will forgive me, I think there is danger of Germany's doing just this, of imposing rules and regulations so drastic that the minds of the young are cramped and hurt." She paused. This was perhaps rather plain talk for a woman in a simple black gown, without even a ring on her finger, to address to a grand duchess and a sovereign. "I hope I haven't offended you."

"Not at all. I asked—"

"And when I'm asked, I answer. Frankness is my habit."

"Your frankness does not offend," said the grand duchess. "I commend it!"

Before Christmas Clara went to Montbeliard and oversaw the provisioning of the town's destitute with a stock of fuel and receipted rent checks for the winter months.

"It's Boston that does this good little thing," she said to Antoinette Margot. "Now I'm going to Strasbourg. I want to be there for the holiday season. Last year my shop workers had a party for me. I was so surprised! This year it's my turn."

That was a party to be remembered always. Three hundred invitations were printed and sent by mail—which in itself was exciting to women who probably never had known the postman to stop at their humble dwellings. The date was Saturday night, December 30. For days before, Clara and Miss Margot bustled about, renting the most spacious hall in Strasbourg, hiring a caterer, buying two enormous trees imported from the Black Forest, ordering twenty cakes and five hundred sugar-and-raisin rolls from the bakeries—and making other, and mysterious, purchases.

In the afternoon of December 30, the trees were erected upon a platform in front of two big mirrors and trimmed with glistening ornaments and waxen tapers. Long tables were laid with white cloths, and the floor spread with moss on which snowflakes of white paper and mica were sprinkled. Boughs of fir and sprays of little scarlet winter berries were massed in the window sills, on the walls, and twined into the branches of the fine glass chandeliers.

The party was scheduled for seven o'clock. But by six-thirty, while Clara and Miss Margot were secretly busy, the guests began to arrive.

"What shall we do?" asked Miss Margot.

"Keep them out of the hall," Clara said. "I'll light the trees."

Promptly at seven the doors were opened; at the same instant the parlor organ, hidden in a bower of hemlock, burst into music. And what an instant it was! The beautiful room, all white and green, with every detail of it and the twinkling candles repeatedly reflected in the mirrors, until the whole world seemed sparkling and radiant.

There was a sigh, a silence, and then a ripple of rapturous exclamations. The guests filed in. The organ played a Christmas hymn and everybody sang; a prayer was said; the platters of cake and baskets of delicious rolls, the pots of steaming fragrant chocolate appeared. Oh, the hubbub of voices!

The evening's climax came when Clara distributed the gifts. Each woman received a morocco purse filled—really filled!—with silver pieces. Amazement was boundless and noisy. They laughed and they cried, and they told themselves and their neighbors at table just how the money would be used. But this discussion had been anticipated, and Miss Margot made a little speech, gently explaining that it was Miss Barton's wish that the money be not squandered but saved, as a nest egg, a starting of a savings account for each family in its new life. The women of Strasbourg had been thrifty in the old days, Miss Margot said. They must be so again. And they agreed: "Yes, yes! We will!"

"Such a time," Clara wrote to her sister Sally. "It was worth going a mile to see!"

Amusingly enough, a second party had to be given. This was much more exclusive, only for those women whose invitations had somehow not reached them. Checking over her list, Clara had missed some of her friends and guessed why they were missing. She was too fond of them all to have a single one slighted. So, three days later, the celebration was restaged—on a smaller scale.

Clara was thinking of home. In the spring she was not well and admitted in a letter to David that she was having a "little difficulty" with her eyes. This was understatement. Her eyes were acutely affected. For weeks they must be bandaged and she had to sit in a dark room in enforced idleness. Her head and throat ached, and she was quite miserable.

She had friends, Mr. and Mrs. Sheldon, in London, who were urging her to come to them. Why should she stay in Germany? Hadn't her first reason for coming abroad been to travel and recuperate? Instead, she had slaved away, eating sparing and unbalanced meals, sleeping at night never more than five hours, and usually much less—day and night spurring herself to almost superhuman effort. The Sheldons would meet her in Paris and take her through Italy and then to England.

Obediently, yet with no exuberance, Clara yielded. She toured Italy, seeing all the sights, and went to London. From there she sailed in August with Miss Margot for a month on the Isle of Wight, just off the southern coast of England.

It was one of the few good vacations of her life, with the sunny beach at the threshold of Clara's pretty little cottage, and the weather delightful and many American and English callers dropping in for the week-ends.

Still Clara thought of home. She knew she was far from normal in health. Perhaps an English winter would strengthen her. And then, surely, next spring she could sail.

"I have something to do there," she said to Miss Margot. "Something imperative!"

But in London where she took lodgings, she was suddenly and alarmingly ill, and for a very long time indeed. Nervous prostration, her physician said. She mustn't contemplate the voyage to America until she had greatly rallied. David sent his daughter Mary to be with her. He would have gone himself, or Sally or Sally's husband or their son or Bernard's wife, Fannie Childs Barton—all were frantic with worry, any or all of them would have gone to her. But Clara would not hear of it: she had the ever-faithful Antoinette beside her; Antoinette and Mary, the dear girls, were quite capable of looking after "the ailing auntie."

Clara wrote often and with a deceptive cheerfulness to her relatives, making light of her condition. She was, in truth, paying the penalty now for those war years in America and in Europe. It was her peculiarity of temperament that in the midst of stress she was buoyed to an astonishing vigor—and when the stress was removed, she sagged like a pricked balloon.

By coincidence, Florence Nightingale, the heroine of the

Crimean War, was also in London that winter of 1872. Clara Barton revered Miss Nightingale, who had earned such honor and fame not only in her native England but also in all the world and had inspired Henry Wadsworth Longfellow to write the lovely poem, *Santa Filomena*. But the two women, of such similar endowments and careers, did not meet, for Florence Nightingale, too, was very sick just then, confined in a nursing home.

Eventually, in October of the following year, Clara sailed for America. As she had said to Antoinette Margot, she felt that she had something imperative beckoning her to another of her beginnings.

She thought of what she had said once to David. "What can one person do?" And of his rejoinder, "More maybe than you know." Perhaps also she thought of the fifteen-year-old Clara, lying—so comically swollen with mumps—on a sofa outside the parlor, and hearing a phrenologist (who might be a psychologist as well, or even a prophet) say to her mother, "Whatever she undertakes, she'll never fail."

22

HEN she came home that autumn of 1873, Clara
Barton wore on the front of her inexpensive dress
the Gold Cross of Remembrance, presented by
the Grand Duke of Baden, and a magnificent amethyst, said
to be one of the finest in the world, given her by the Grand
Duchess Louise. In her satchel were the Jewel of the Red Cross,
from Queen Natalie of Serbia, and the Iron Cross of Merit,
awarded by the Emperor and Empress of Germany. From
France she had no decorations—except the love and gratitude
of the lowly thousands to whom she had ministered.

She went to Washington, then to Oxford. There she was
joined by Antoinette Margot.

"I followed you," Miss Margot said. "I had the feeling you
were not well. I thought you might need me."

And beyond doubt Clara did need her, or someone, or
something. "I don't know what's the matter with me, Antoinette," she said sadly. "I'm not myself. Shall I ever be again?
This nervous trouble, whatever it is—I don't know where
I'll find the cure for it."

She found that finally at Dansville, New York. Years earlier,
lecturing, Clara had gone to Dansville. A sanatorium was
there, much advertised and which attracted patients from
every state in the Union. For the first months Clara lived in
the sanatorium proper. With summer she bought a house of
her own near by and settled down to an invalid's existence.

It was, of course, one to which she was by disposition badly suited, consisting of much rest in bed, mild exercising, wholesome food, absolute freedom from responsibility, and quiet. Her recreations were only those of the sanatorium parlors: sedate musicales, evenings of stereopticon slides; soothing sermons on Sundays. As an invalid she was withdrawn from contact with current affairs, politics, or any of the subjects in which she had once been so absorbed. She could read—but nothing that would irritate the emotions or stimulate the intellect. She could bring her journal up to date. Sometimes she composed verses which she recited at village functions. A cotton-batting existence, and she loathed it!

Dansville was proud to have for a resident this woman of renown. On Memorial Day, several hundred Dansville folk accorded her an ovation, a procession winding to the sanatorium, with waving flags, a brass band, flowery speeches, the singing of the *Star-Spangled Banner,* and nosegays heaped about her feet as she sat, utterly astonished, on the veranda. She was touched by the tribute, embarrassed—and preoccupied.

A prominent New York publisher visited her and asked her to write her memoirs. Because he seemed to wish it so much, she said she would, and she did sketch a tentative chapter or two. But how silly, she thought, to be writing about herself. ("As if I were already dead, my usefulness over!") Was it for this she had returned to her native land?

As a matter of fact, though she had submitted to the doctors' verdict and instructions and seemed bent upon nothing else than growing strong, though her surface might be unruffled, inwardly she seethed and fumed. Not for a moment had she forgotten that morning at dawn in a German camp when she had made, to herself and (she believed) to God and all His creatures, a solemn vow. Now she was being kept from redeeming it, and she chafed at the restraint.

In 1877 the American newspapers reported what seemed to be another European war in the brewing, this time between Russia and Turkey. Clara Barton was progressing toward health then; she could see people, converse, walk about. She knew that, in the event of a new upheaval there, she could not go abroad, nor did she want to, yet the thought of the war obsessed her.

"If it comes, America will be asked to care for the sufferers. Is not this the moment for the organization of which I've dreamed?"

She wrote to Dr. Appia and to Monsieur Gustave Moynier in Switzerland and told them what was in her mind: the forming of an American Red Cross. Thus far, her ideas were rather indefinite, but they included a national headquarters with smaller units in every state and perhaps an integrated net which would reach out even to the tiniest hamlet. America was so big, so impulsive and open-handed. But always its charities had lacked system.

She closed her letter with the timid inquiry whether the Convention would wish her to attempt any such organization.

Both Dr. Appia and Monsieur Moynier replied. They said they had lamented the previous stand of the United States, the failure of Dr. Bellows of the Sanitary Commission. But, yes, certainly the time was now ripe for another crusade. And who but Miss Barton was so qualified to lead it? What other man or woman had seen the Red Cross operating on the field, behind the battle line? Her Swiss friends would do everything they could to aid her.

Dr. Appia was a realist. He said Miss Barton must concentrate on three objectives: the influencing of public opinion in America; the gaining of the President's approval; and, most important, the securing of adoption by the Senate of the Geneva treaty. To Clara in Dansville he sent a letter written by Monsieur Moynier and addressed to President Rutherford B. Hayes.

"This letter," he said to Clara, "you must deliver immediately, in person." And he added that it contained the information of Clara Barton's appointment to head the American branch of the International Red Cross.

It was strange (or was it?) how Clara reacted to the assignment. Her invalid's lassitude seemed to fall from her like a cast-off robe for which she now had no necessity. She felt sturdy, fit for anything. Once more she had a specific task before her. And she was ready for it, well!

Also, though she did not know it, she was confronting the most involved and arduous struggle of her life.

Monsieur Moynier's letter was written in French. Clara translated it. She had always thought one barrier to American appreciation of the Geneva Convention's aims was that its literature was in a language foreign to Americans. In January 1878, with the letter, she went to Washington.

President Hayes was out of town, but Congress was in session. Unwilling to waste precious weeks, Clara made a round of calls on those officials and Congressmen with whom she was acquainted. And she wrote and had printed a pamphlet: *What the Red Cross Is.* In it she set forth the provisions of the Geneva treaty: ". . . for the neutrality of all sanitary supplies, ambulances, surgeons, nurses, attendants, sick or wounded men, and their safe-conduct, when they bear the sign of the organization, viz., the Red Cross." She traced the steps by which the society had matured and told of its testing in the Franco-Prussian War, its centralization and impartiality.

And she added a quite remarkable clause, one which was the fruit of her own thinking, and solely of that, one of which Dr. Appia and Monsieur Moynier never even had spoken:

". . . It may be further made a part of the *raison d'être* of these national relief societies to afford ready succor and assistance to sufferers in time of national or widespread calamities, such as plagues, cholera, yellow fever and the like, devastating fires or floods, railway disasters, mining catastrophes, etc. . . ."

Thus she had broadened the scope of Red Cross principles— in a way which would have results.

President Hayes was a hard man to see; finally, she got an audience with him. He was courteous enough, but, alas, how evasive. Had not the Red Cross been previously considered? And American assent withheld? Well, then— But he would refer Miss Barton to other officials.

Some of these men were apathetic. The Red Cross? They'd never heard of it. Anyway, why bother with it now?

"We'll never have war again in this country, Miss Barton."

"God grant that. I've observed war—more closely perhaps, and for a longer period, than you have. I know what it's like. I pray for peace and all that may promote it. But when I stop and think—I fear."

"No, no, Miss Barton! You are a woman, with the frailty of your sex."

She smiled covertly at that, knowing quite a lot about the frailty of her sex. "Unfortunately," she said, "there are crises during peace times, too. No country is so liable as ours to overmastering adversities. I wish it weren't so, but seldom a year goes by that we aren't brought to consternation by some unforeseen hardship in some section of the continent. Like war, these things are out of the common course; like death they're certain to strike, though we may not know how or when or where. We should be as a family, all united and prepared to go to the rescue of any one member."

"We do that now. We're a Good Samaritan sort of people."

"We must do it intelligently and economically. With system rather than extravagance and makeshifts. I've seen the Good Samaritans, too. Untrained, they lose thousands of dollars by their bungling and duplications, funds slip through their fingers."

"Well, maybe you know what you're about, Miss Barton. But you've tackled an uphill business."

Other officials were openly hostile. They rated Clara Barton as just one more fanatic reformer.

"Chatter. Nothing but chatter. You'll never get anywhere with that scheme. Doesn't the Monroe Doctrine warn us against entangling alliances?"

As the months lagged by and all her entreaties seemed to fall upon deaf ears, and President Hayes remained aloof and would not see her again, Clara sustained herself with the hope that her pamphlet might plead for her. But with the year's ending she acknowledged that it hadn't. She had perused every newspaper to be had in Washington and New England. Her family and her friends had been vigilantly watching for some comment—if only a paragraph, a line. There was none. Apparently not one man, woman, or child anywhere had read it, ever, a single time.

"I mailed so many copies," she mused ruefully, "and I might just as well have dropped them down a cistern." She realized now why Dr. Bellows had been discouraged. An uphill business? "But I shall never admit that it's futile. Never." She smiled a little. "Nobody can be so stubborn as a Barton."

In the last days of President Hayes' term of office she closed her Dansville house and moved to Washington. "I'll stay here, right on the ground, and see this thing through."

James A. Garfield would be the next President. Clara had frequently encountered him during the Civil War, of which he was a veteran. He was a statesman with an eloquent tongue, a scholar who in his penurious youth had been a teacher in the schools of Ohio. Early privations had given Garfield the viewpoint of the humanitarian.

With his election, Clara's hope revived.

23

T HROUGH the breezy brightness of an early spring morning in 1881, Clara walked to her appointment with President Garfield. Her friend had occupied his exalted office as the nation's Chief Executive just a month. She had made her request for an hour of his valuable time so urgent that it could not be ignored. In the past year she had learned much of the ways of functionaries and red-tapists and had cooled her heels in many an anteroom, where she was admonished to wait and be very patient. Henceforth, her watchword would be to take time by the forelock, to depend on no one but herself.

She would see the President personally in face-to-face interview—and she had dressed for the occasion. She wore her best shoes, gown, and hat; the coat, quite fashionable, of green worsted with immense mink-trimmed sleeves and collar, she had borrowed from Fannie Childs Barton, because her own coat was so shabby. She carried a leather case which contained a copy of her pamphlet and other papers, and an umbrella. (You never can tell about the April weather.)

She liked the Washington which she saw about her. It had always seemed to her the most exciting city in the world, breathing vitality. Now it was attaining beauty and grandeur. The dome of the Capitol had been completed and surmounted with Thomas Crawford's towering bronze statue of Freedom.

The building of the Washington Monument had been resumed and the obelisk of marble was climbing skyward; ornamental trees were planted along paths and drives, and parks were landscaped. To Clara this growth seemed evidence of the country's solid foundations and its reach for immortality.

She went up the curved lane, between the elms, to the White House portico and there was ushered into the hall and then into the East Room, with its mirrored walls and shining parquet floor. She sat down on a gilt-and-damask bench, conscious of the thumping of her heart. She had been in the mansion before, never without the sensation of intense pride in its simplicity and dignity. She heard the door opening, a foot on the threshold.

"Miss Barton?"

"Mr. President."

He came quickly to her and clasped her hand. "This is a pleasure. Since we last met you have added new laurels to your coronet. You and your talents—and perhaps also the virtues of our American tradition as good neighbors—now have a reputation beyond the seas."

"You mean what little I accomplished in France? It's that I want to discuss with you," she said. "I have a letter for you, Mr. President." She got the envelope out of the leather case. "The original is rather soiled; it was intended for your predecessor. But here's a translation, freshly written." She offered a second envelope.

"I'm to read this?"

"At once, if you will. There's been much delay, and every day counts."

As he unfolded the paper, she sat in silence, her eyes resting on his bald head, strong features, and bulky shoulders.

"Yes, we cannot afford to be excluded." He glanced up,

nodding. "You must call upon Mr. Blaine, the Secretary of State."

"When, sir?"

"Today. Tell him that your project is assured of my co-operation in every phase."

James G. Blaine strode into the Diplomatic Chamber at the Capitol. He was tall and handsome, white-haired and white-bearded, one of the most magnetic figures ever to cross the American political scene. Later he would be dubbed "the plumed knight of Maine," Robert Ingersoll's sobriquet for him as a Presidential nominee in the campaign of 1884. But to Clara Barton, little and demure in her borrowed finery, Blaine was an unknown quantity and, so often rebuffed, she wondered what to expect from him. Would he second Garfield's approval?

"I'm sorry, Miss Barton, to have kept you waiting," he said, bowing.

"You know why I'm here, Mr. Secretary?"

"I have a memorandum on my desk, yes. I confess though that I'm woefully ignorant about the Red Cross. Will you briefly outline it?" He listened carefully and then said, "I had thought it was an *American* society. The international angle hadn't occurred to me."

"But that's—well, it's everything!" She hesitated. Had she, at the start, forfeited his interest? Statesmen were wary of foreign entanglements. Yet it was precisely this, to enlist America in a movement which embraced all races and lands and united them in a philanthropic brotherhood which was her goal. Mr. Blaine seemed to be turning away, and she was desperate with the thought that her opportunity, so dearly bought, was slipping from her. "Oh, if only I didn't have to be *brief!*"

His smile was charming. "You may have all the time you wish, Miss Barton, all there is."

She told him then the whole story, even going back to what had been her dream at Antietam, at the Lacy House in Falmouth, at Belle Plain, where inefficiency had marooned thousands of poor wretches hub deep in a morass of mud and rain. She told him of Dr. Appia's coming to her in Geneva and of her surprise at his announcements, and of how, with a swiftness which smacked of the dramatic, she had witnessed a theory enacted as a practice. She mentioned Strasbourg, Lyon, Belfort, Paris, after the siege; in each instance, organization had substituted life for death, order for chaos.

"Mr. Blaine, I promised myself—and more, I promised the representatives of other countries—that I would spend every ounce of my effort toward the securing of the signature of the United States to the Geneva treaty. And that I would secure it."

"Why did not President Hayes subscribe to the treaty?"

"His objections were mainly that it had been once rejected and thus must be worthless, and also that it would not be consistent with the Monroe Doctrine."

"But the Monroe Doctrine was not made to ward off humanity, Miss Barton." Secretary Blaine paused. "The signing would be a matter for the United States Senate, as you probably know. Well, since you have the President's commendation, I daresay the Senate's, too, could be had. And I agree with President Garfield: Obviously this is a thing in which we should have a part with other nations. If we did not, it might be to our everlasting discredit—"

"Oh, I am so glad you think of it like that!" She could not

restrain the exclamation. She flushed. "I see it all so clearly. And the Red Cross not only needs us, but we need it. Fifty years ago we could, perhaps, preserve an isolation and maintain our old attitude of being entirely self-sufficient. But as a people we are changing, Mr. Blaine, and that's inevitable, what with the industrial expansion and the settlement of the West, our inventions and manufactories and enormous commerce. Now we must meet the modern times with modern institutions, and the Red Cross would be in the forefront of these. It should be large in its scope and narrowing down to take in even the smallest community and the individuals who make up that community. When the organization has been perfected —and notice, Mr. Blaine, that I say *when* and not *if*—it will be headed by the President of the United States, and there will be millions of names on its roster, many of them the names of the humble and obscure. For I have found that no one group among our citizenry has a monopoly on kindness. It's everywhere, often in the most unlikely places, and every fellow countryman of ours has been touched with it. The Red Cross will furnish a vehicle for the expression of that kindness." She stopped. "My enthusiasm is running away with me."

"It is contagious, Miss Barton. It will be a factor in your ultimate success."

"Then you really do think I'll succeed?"

"Have you yourself ever doubted it?" ·

"No," she said honestly. "Never."

"What allies have you?"

"None as yet. I've worked—and prayed—alone."

Secretary Blaine wrote something on a card. "Present this tomorrow to Mr. Robert T. Lincoln, the Secretary of War."

More elated than she had been in many months, Clara went through the Corinthian columns of the Capitol corridors, down

the long flight of steps, down the terrace, and along the Mall.
It was drizzling a bit; she put up her umbrella.

"Mr. Lincoln," she said, "I knew your father. I had the
privilege of establishing a bureau for him."

"To identify the missing soldiers of the Civil War, Miss
Barton?"

"Yes. So much has been said in praise of Abraham Lincoln
that anything I might add would be trite and repetitious. Yet—
I knew him, I talked with him. I worked with and for him.
Those are memories of which I can never be robbed, to treasure
always."

Abraham Lincoln's distinguished son inclined his head.
"Thank you. My father had confidence in you, Miss Barton.
I have the same confidence. I will support the Red Cross
wherever I can. I believe in it."

She went from one to another of the Cabinet members and
was cordially received. All official Washington seemed suddenly alert to her message. Each day she made dozens of calls,
on Senators, Representatives, on anyone who might be a convert. Secretary Blaine formally replied to Monsieur Moynier,
pledging American sympathy in "the amelioration of the
suffering incident to warfare" and the favoring by the Administration of Congressional adoption of the international
treaty.

Clara's hopes were soaring. She forgot she ever had been
ill or distraught or worried. So optimistic was she that on
May 21, she held a meeting and actually organized the "Association of the American Red Cross," which was duly and
properly incorporated under the laws of the District of Columbia, with a board composed of prominent men—judges,

doctors, army officers—and two women, one of them Clara herself. She had asked James A. Garfield to be its president, but he declined. Clara Barton must be president, he said, and he nominated her for that honor.

The American Red Cross was now a fact—or almost. It had the President's consent, Mr. Blaine and Mr. Lincoln as advocates; the Senators seemed to be in unanimous accord. Nothing hindered consummation except the signing of the treaty. That would soon be obtained.

Clara remembered what Dr. Appia had said of the value of publicity. She had no press committee. Perhaps she must attend herself to this detail.

One summer night she sat up in bed, lighted her candle, and took a pencil and a three-penny pad from the table. Out of the fullness of her heart she began to write *A Sketch of the Red Cross*—another pamphlet, an appeal to the people, a labor of love. At dawn she was still scribbling.

That was the morning of July 2, 1881, clear, hot—tranquil. President Garfield was leaving for a holiday. With Secretary Blaine, other Cabinet members and their wives, and a few more friends, he was taking a special train to New York, where he would meet Mrs. Garfield and his sons and his daughter, Mollie. From New York the party would range through New England, stopping at Williamstown, Massachusetts, to attend the graduation exercises of Williams College, of which the President was an alumnus, stopping also in Augusta, Maine, at the home of the Blaines. It would be the pleasantest of trips.

President Garfield rode out of the White House grounds in a carriage, with Secretary Blaine beside him. The coachman reined his horses at the Sixth Street portal of the Baltimore & Potomac railroad station.

"Here we are, sir," the coachman said, tipping his hat.

Officer Kearney was the policeman on duty at the station that morning. In his neat uniform and visored cap, Kearney had been patrolling the premises. He knew the President's party was expected and that perhaps a little group of people might assemble for a glimpse of the great men and their ladies. Kearney had often seen the President. It was a joy to see and to serve him, for Garfield was so genial, always smiling.

On his rounds Kearney noticed someone—an idler who for an hour had been dodging in and out of the building. Kearney looked at the chap. He was slender and short, with sunken cheeks, sandy mustache, chin whiskers tinged with gray; he had his slouch hat pulled down over his eyes, his hands in the pockets of his blue serge suit.

Kearney was near enough to hear what he said to a hackman: "Can I be driven away from here in a hurry—if it's necessary?"

"That's funny," Kearney thought. "Wonder what *he's* up to?"

He might have made a point of asking the little man. But just then the White House carriage rolled to the curb. Kearney sprang to open the carriage door.

"Good morning, Officer." The President leaned out. "How much time have we?"

"About ten minutes, sir." Kearney was rigorously at attention.

For several of the ten minutes, Mr. Garfield and Mr. Blaine lounged, talking, in the carriage. Then they got out and, arm in arm, very leisurely, went through the ladies' waiting room and into the general passengers' foyer.

A shot split the drone of many voices, the tread of many feet. And another shot. At the first detonation the President whirled toward Mr. Blaine; the bullet had torn his right coat sleeve. But with the second, the President fell heavily to the floor.

Mr. Blaine gasped, stooped over the prostrate form, straightened, turned to the entrance, where a man in a slouch hat was plunging into the rapidly gathering crowd, a smoking pistol in his grasp.

"Get him! Get that man!"

But Officer Kearney already had got him. There was never any likelihood of an escape. An hour later, Charles J. Guiteau was lodged in the Washington jail.

The ambulance passed slowly along the streets and the crowd slowly followed. "The President has been assassinated." Amazement was in the cry which echoed the length and breadth of the city, and disbelief, horror. Then an uncanny hush settled; through it the ambulance went to the White House, where the ponderous gates opened and then shut, and soldier sentinels suddenly appeared as if by magic, in a cordon inside the iron fence.

He was conscious. As the ambulance halted, he glanced up at familiar faces of servants peering from the upper windows. He raised his right hand in military salute. "Long live the Republic!"

They carried him to a southeast bedroom. Doctors and nurses encircled him. His one thought was for his wife, and he dictated a telegram:

The President wishes me to say to you from him that he has been seriously hurt—how seriously he cannot yet say. He is himself, and hopes you will come to him soon. He sends his love to you.

Between the seizures of pain, he was cheerful.

"Blaine, what motive do you think that man could have had in trying to assassinate me?"

"I do not know, Mr. President. He says he had no motive. He must be insane."

Garfield smiled. "I suppose he thought it would be a glorious thing to emulate the pirate chief."

Blaine did not repeat the already current gossip, that this man was a disgruntled seeker after a government post, a consulship—the same irrational eccentric and religious crank who a week earlier had forced his way into Garfield's presence and made himself so obnoxious that he must be forcibly ousted, or that the crime had been plotted for an earlier date and been deferred. "I am a lawyer," Guiteau was declaring pompously to his jailers, "a theologian and a politician."

The President was brave. "Conceal nothing from me," he begged. "I am not afraid to die. Tell me frankly."

"Mr. President," the doctor said, "your condition is extremely critical. I do not think you can live many hours."

"God's will be done, Doctor. I'm ready to go if my time has come."

It had not come; not quite. In the evening he heard the sound of wheels on the drive. "That's my wife! My boys, and Mollie. Now I shall sleep."

He slept until midnight. "There is just a chance," the doctor said.

"Then, Doctor, we must take that chance."

Weeks, months, all through the summer he lingered, while the country prayed, and despaired, and prayed again. He had good days and bad. Always he was serene, his manner reassuring, even playful. His courage was superb, never wavering, an example to the world.

Everything was done for him that science could do. Alexander Graham Bell invented an apparatus which by electrical devices located the bullet beneath the ribs. The machine was somewhat like Bell's telephone, which he was then perfecting. But the surgeons deemed it unwise to probe for the treacherous bit of lead until the President should be stronger.

On September 6, they moved him from the searing heat of Washington to his seaside cottage at Elberon, New Jersey. His chamber looked directly out on the beach. Propped up with pillows, he could watch the thundering green surf.

On September 19, he died there.

Vice President Chester A. Arthur took the oath as President at one-thirty in the morning, in the parlor of his private residence. Next day the ceremony was re-enacted in the Capitol, with Chief Justice Waite of the Supreme Court administering the oath and ex-Presidents Hayes and Grant, General William T. Sherman, the Cabinet members, and a few Senators and Representatives standing near.

Deeply affected, with trembling voice, Arthur spoke briefly, asserting his determination to further the policies of Garfield. Perhaps Arthur was remembering something which James A. Garfield himself had said in 1865 when Abraham Lincoln died:

"God reigns, and the government at Washington still lives."

At that moment on the President's desk, as yet unsigned, lay Clara Barton's Geneva treaty.

24

CLARA had been spending the summer in Dansville. It was there that the news of Garfield's death reached her. For a while she was utterly despondent. She had put her heart and soul into the tedious, wearisome struggle to get the Red Cross formulated. And was it all to be done over again now? She thought of many things. Would it be better if she turned the matter into someone else's hands? Yet there was no one who cared as she did. There was no one who cared at all. Maybe she ought to give up the idea of the treaty and simply make the Red Cross into a private organization, a pet charity like so many others, with patrons among the wealthy. This, though, was quite at variance with her convictions. No, the Red Cross must belong to the government and the people of the United States. It must be theirs, inseparable from their existence. "To my unsophisticated mind," she told a friend, "the government of my country *is* my country, and the *people* of my country are the government."

But the summer had held one incident which cheered her. On August 22, the first local chapter of the Red Cross was effected in Dansville. It was the eighteenth anniversary of the drawing of the Geneva treaty in Switzerland. Clara had presided, and for that evening, at least, she had felt jubilant.

And the next month was eventful—probably more important to Clara than she realized at the time. For then occurred such a disaster as she often had cited in her pleadings.

215

In eastern Michigan were white pine forests. The region had been settled by thrifty immigrant farmers, Poles, Scandinavians, Canadians, and a sprinkling of pioneering New Englanders, who cleared vast tracts among the trees. During the drought of July and August, 1881, the farmers burned the stumps and the brush from the acres they were cultivating.

On September 4, the sky above Sanilac County was murky with smoke. On September 5, the wind from Lake Huron's shores fanned up a sheet of flame which streaked viciously inland and would not be controlled.

The newspapers were full of Michigan's plight. Five thousand homeless; stock, crops, barns, fences, reduced to smoldering embers, feathery ash. These people must have help!

It was the cue for the Dansville Red Cross Society and for the Rochester and Syracuse branches, which instantly organized. A white and scarlet banner was unfurled over the Dansville chapter's rooms—the first display of the Red Cross flag in America. And Clara had not mistaken the spirit of the town: gifts of food and clothing poured in upon her.

She dispatched the packing cases to Michigan, and then she caught the train which would meet the supplies at their destination. In her purse were three thousand dollars—her own contribution to the stricken. There were other dispensers of goods and money, but none more valiant than the wearers of the Red Cross emblem.

Returning to New York, Clara learned that there had been much editorial comment. Perhaps this new movement was a pretty praiseworthy thing. It was for wartime relief, yes. But it contained a clause for the relief of national emergencies also. And it had proved that it could achieve results.

Now the pamphlet Clara had written was being read—with interest, tinged faintly with surprise. Newspapers and periodicals reviewed it. Clara had more than five hundred clippings for her scrapbook.

Still, the treaty had not been ratified by the United States Senate.

Early in November Clara attended the trial of Guiteau in the Criminal Court of the District of Columbia, where the assassin was sanely arguing that he was insane. Afterward, she went to the White House to see President Arthur.

She had known him for several years and was impressed with his amiability and good looks. Once in the halls of the Capitol he had stopped her and expressed his sympathy for the Red Cross. She reminded him of that now.

"Mr. President, the United States is committed to the treaty; Mr. Blaine avowed our intentions in a letter to Monsieur Moynier. If we repudiate it, we will seem absurd in the eyes of the other parties. And there are twenty-five of them at present. Twenty-five signers. If we hurry we can be the twenty-sixth!"

The irony was not lost on him. He smiled. "Miss Barton, I know you are sorry for Mr. Blaine's resignation from the Cabinet. You will miss him. But he has not forgotten you. Mr. Blaine already has spoken to Mr. Frederick Frelinghuysen, the new Secretary of State, about your treaty. Nor have I forgotten, either. I have had an official request from the Senate for information regarding the treaty, and I have had printed everything available on the subject and am sending this to the Senate. I expect to affix my own signature at the earliest possible moment. But these preliminaries take time, Miss Barton. We must be like Job, resolute and unperturbed."

Like Job? Clara believed that she could have beaten that badgered patriarch at his own chastening game.

She stayed in Washington. The winter seemed long and sad

and dreary, and it brought another complication. Rival organizations sprang up here and there, perhaps a dozen of them, each one flaunting its merit and decrying Clara's work.

The first of these, headed by the "Organizer and Supreme Commander," a gentleman born in England, declared itself to be the only true and original Red Cross and issued a magazine to say that "it is rather late for Miss Barton, or anyone else, to talk about organizing the Red Cross," that the "Supreme Commander's" society had been in existence since 1879. Already a "Grand Promenade Concert" had been given in honor of the leader, who was girding himself for some great action along humanitarian lines; more concerts would surely follow.

Clara had a sense of humor. She could, and did, laugh at this bombast. But one rival of the Red Cross had money and influence behind it, and grew to such proportions that it threatened to eclipse all the rest. And Clara was sorely troubled. If the "White Cross," or any group which had named itself so similarly, became sturdy enough to endure, would there then be place for the Red Cross? The "White Cross," and some of the other organizations, might be worthy. Probably they were, and their backers were conscientious folk. Yet none, Clara felt, had the scope of her own organization, none had its foundations laid upon so broad a plan and the difficult groundwork already completed. Besides, it was to her and to no other person that Monsieur Moynier had spoken. He had wanted her as the medium through which the American branch would be drawn into the international whole. For years she had been toiling, until the Red Cross had become the most precious thing in her life. Now that success seemed at least a possibility, was it not natural and right that she should wish to share it?

Her courage was drained by these annoyances. Not even the cheering word from her bankers, that her own financial affairs had prospered and her annual income considerably increased, could dispel the gloom of her spirit. She need never worry so far as the means of livelihood were concerned. But for the Red Cross, the treaty, she worried constantly.

She believed, too, that she perceived a veering in the tide of public opinion. Was it a fact, or did she imagine, that obstacles were bobbing up to hinder the treaty? She knew there was dissension in the Senate. Perhaps the treaty would be involved somehow in a political snarl—and tossed out, obliterated. Such conjectures haunted her. She could not eat or sleep at night. How terrible, she thought, to be dependent upon the will of other persons, many other persons. If only this were a task which she could do alone.

A February morning came when she was nearer despair than ever before. "It did not seem like other days," she wrote afterward. "There was either much to do or nothing to do." For so long the fate of the thing she most desired had hung in the balance. Now a few hours must decide it. But the doubt and the postponements were intolerable, the having to be passive when she had been always energetic.

And why must she be so? Hadn't she a great deal else than that treaty to live for? She would wash her hands of it and forget it!

The weather was damp and cold and gray, but she had the impulse to tramp for miles, to exert and tire herself. She donned an old hat, a mackintosh, galoshes, and went outdoors. At the corner she hesitated. Which direction? Not downtown! She would not approach the Capitol or its environs; of that she was positive. She wouldn't inquire further about the treaty.

Because she didn't care. Let the secretaries and the Senators do as they pleased. Clara Barton was sheering away from any responsibility. She was free!

Buttoning her coat collar, she set off at a brisk pace—toward the Capitol.

She went to the State Department.

"Is Mr. Frelinghuysen in?"

Yes, he was in, and hastening to greet her.

"Miss Barton! I was just going to send a messenger for you."

"For me? Why?"

"I have something to show you." The Secretary of State was an affable young man, smooth-shaven except for a ruffle of blond whiskers under his chin. "Step into my office." He piloted her in and shut the door and whispered conspiratorially, "Would you like to see the treaty?"

"I would." Her voice was very small, very wistful.

He opened a drawer and from it extracted a volume, a kind of unbound book, fourteen inches square, of soft parchment. He laid it in her lap. Trembling, she fingered the pages. It was a solemn and historic document, and she could not read it, her eyes were too misted with sudden tears.

Mr. Frelinghuysen was bending over her. "Does it mean so much to you?" he asked gently.

"It means—everything. You don't know. I—I can't explain."

"The President will sign it tomorrow," he said. "Here is the space for his signature. Then it goes to the Senate, where it will be read and referred to the Committee on Foreign Relations. Then in just about two weeks the Great Seal of the United States will be placed—right here."

She stared blindly at the page he indicated, and a tear coursed down her cheek and splashed on the exact spot where the seal of the United States would be.

"Does it suit you, Miss Barton?"

"It's—wonderful. But I am ashamed of myself for behaving like this."

"Ashamed?" Mr. Frelinghuysen laughed. "My dear lady! My dear Miss Barton!"

On the night of March 16, 1882, a note was delivered to her. It was from the Senate Chamber, from a Senator who was her devoted friend:

Miss Barton:

I have the gratifying privilege of informing you of the ratification by the Senate of the Geneva Convention; of the full assent of the United States to the same, by the action of the Senate this afternoon. I had the injunction of secrecy removed so that it could be published at once. The whole is in print, and if I get time I will send you some copies in the morning. . . .

LAUS DEO!

Very truly,

E. S. LAPHAM.

It was done!

The mails were too slow to carry such a glorious announcement. Clara cabled to Monsieur Moynier and to Dr. Appia. Then for hours she stood at her window, looking out into the darkness, her forehead against the pane.

She knew that the moment her cablegram was received there would be a burst of celebration in a dozen European cities, bonfires lighted in the streets and people singing.

Washington was quiet—as if nothing extraordinary had happened. No excitement here, no demonstration of rejoicing. Only one woman, slender and silent and solitary, keeping a vigil. But her eyes were alight and her heart was singing.

25

THE American Red Cross was now an actuality. Perhaps some skeptics had supposed that once the treaty was ratified, Clara Barton would seek a Congressional appropriation for the expenses of organization. But this was not the case. At the outset she had said, and was often to reiterate, "The Red Cross means not national aid for the needs of the people, but the people's aid for the needs of the Nation." She would not accept a salary or permit any friend of hers in Congress to introduce a bill for her financial advantage. As for extending the organization, she trusted to the enthusiasm of public sentiment, which had noted the functioning of the Red Cross in Michigan. Now several local chapters were forming; she knew there would be many more.

But the work, as Clara then saw it, was for intervals of emergency only, and therefore would not occupy all the time of a person like herself, who enjoyed being strenuously busy. She was the president of the Red Cross—and how proud she was to be that! She proposed to keep in closest touch with it. But she rather coveted the opportunity to show that she was entirely self-supporting and had not promoted the Red Cross because she lacked other employment. She had appointed Dr. Julian Hubbell as her field agent and had named other subordinate officers, with whom she could be in almost instantaneous communication if emergency presented. In the autumn of 1882, she began to look for something else to do, a salaried position, which would take her out of Washington for a while.

This position she found, astonishingly enough, when in January 1883 Governor Butler of Massachusetts proferred her the superintendency of the Massachusetts Woman's Reformatory at Sherborn.

The matron of a prison? It was certainly not what she ever had pictured herself. Yet the work would pay her $1,500 a year. Besides, Governor Butler was urging her to try it. As a Civil War general, Benjamin F. Butler had been her constant friend. She must always remember his thoughtfulness to her when Stephen was so ill in Virginia. Thereafter, the cordiality between Butler and all the Bartons had never waned. Clara felt now that she must be mindful of the accumulated obligations.

So, somewhat reluctantly, she said that she would go to Sherborn.

Her going was deferred several months because of the Mississippi River flood in the early spring, which was followed by the tornado that hit Louisiana. In both disasters the Red Cross performed ably. It was a vital organ of national relief ("the heart," Clara said); its efficiency thrived in the exercising. Dr. Hubbell was alert and practical, Clara was resourceful. As a result, the South manifested its appreciation of the young organization by building up chapters in New Orleans, Memphis, Vicksburg, and other cities in the states which bordered the Mississippi River.

At last, in May, she assumed her duties at the reformatory. "The most foolhardy step," she called it, "of my life."

It was, indeed, a curious and incongruous interlude.

The Sherborn reformatory was reputed to be modern, a model of its kind. But Clara's first reactions, and all her subsequent ones, were of intense pity for the three hundred convicts.

She regarded them as ignorant and misguided rather than sinning. They had been molded by conditions of which they were the hapless victims. They had yielded to temptations. But, she wondered, how different were they from herself? Greatly—or not much? In like circumstances, mightn't she have yielded to the same temptations? Perhaps these women should be penalized, but a better correction would reach back into the homes from which they had come. And Clara knew that such a wholesale reform was obviously impossible.

Almost at once she recognized her inability to cope with the problems of Sherborn, to produce any permanent improvements. She was a misfit, she hadn't the required training. Just one thing prevented her immediate resignation: she had given Governor Butler her word that she would remain for six months.

Well, for that period, at least, this would be not a house of punishment but one of instruction and character development.

With deep thought and fervent prayers she studied the prison rules. Many of them she enforced, some she modified; a few she set aside as not consistent with her program. She varied the institution's routine, and to every woman there she extended her sympathetic understanding.

To such treatment the inmates responded thankfully. She could be firm—and was often, when firmness was in order; and she was respected for that. But she was patient and fair. For these qualities she was beloved. Her charges could talk to her at any time, about anything, and be sure of her interest, and she would transmit their legitimate complaints to the Board of Managers and see that justice was done.

Governor Butler's term in office was drawing to an end. Clara knew that with it her days at Sherborn would end, too. Early in 1884 she went out from the grim walls—gladly, knowing that, though she had been scrupulous and faithful, this was not her proper sphere.

Years later she said, "I have never seen a face there since. I have never returned, and I have no desire to."

She might have said as truthfully that she was a specialist in philanthropic endeavor and the Red Cross was her obsession. Her genius was for that—and perhaps for nothing else.

There had been heavy snows in the Middle West that winter. In February the spring thaw swelled the Ohio River to mammoth size. All the length of the valley the waters rose and were rapidly at flood stage; the countryside from Pittsburgh to the Ohio's juncture with the Mississippi, and beyond, was inundated. The Ohio became a monster, devouring bottomland meadows and pastures, scaling the bluffs to swallow towns and cities. Hundreds of thousands of people were swept from their dwellings and watched their possessions floating away over churning, muddy yellow expanses. The heavens opened and torrents of rain fell, and every dawn brought such a view, of wave and wind and wreckage, as might have greeted Noah.

This was a catastrophe six hundred miles long and forty broad, and Congress voted a large sum for its alleviation. Yet money in itself was not a solution. There must be work! And what more inevitable than that the newly organized American Red Cross (a party to the international treaty of Geneva, if you please!) should undertake the work?

With a handful of volunteers, Clara hastened to Cincinnati. The streets of the city were like canals, pavements completely submerged, skiffs and flatboats plying up and down. Clara rented warehouses which would be distribution centers. She stocked and staffed them, with the good citizens of Cincinnati enthusiastically co-operating. Then she went on down the Ohio to Evansville, that picturesque and historic town in the pocket of southern Indiana.

At Evansville she chartered a steamer, the *Josh V. Throop,* and with the Red Cross flag flying from the masthead and the decks laden with a prodigious cargo, she sailed out upon the flood. In five days she had patrolled the river southwestward to Cairo, Illinois, stopping frequently, wherever a sufferer beckoned, to parcel out medicines, food, clothing, fuel, cash. The weather was by turns sullen or violent; a small cyclone struck and leveled every object which still reared above the water, uprooting trees, whirling houses and barns like cockleshells into the current, multiplying the difficulties of relief a hundredfold.

At Cairo, Clara replenished her supplies, which had been gradually exhausted, and swerved about. She started up the river again in a devious course, shuttling from side to side, from Illinois village to Kentucky village, weaving an intricate pattern of rescue. The *Josh V. Throop,* that strange, cumbersome, crusading craft, excited the interest of newspapers everywhere, and stories which were almost a daily log of its voyage hummed over telegraph wires to blossom forth in print. Clara's slogan of "ready money for instant relief, no paid officers, no solicited funds, no red tape, instantaneous action" captured the Yankee imagination and won wide praise. In a dozen localities societies got together and petitioned for admission into the Red Cross.

For three weeks the *Josh V. Throop* traversed the Ohio, skirting its whirlpools, threading its waste, moving with a ponderous and slightly comic dignity between the drifting ruins of battered farmhouses, drowned sheds and errant chicken coops. The weather cleared, days were short and sunny; at night the moon beamed upon the steamer's blunt smokestacks and silvered the spray of its chugging wheel.

As Clara had foreseen, the deluge of the Ohio made the Mississippi rise to heights which threatened the stoutest levees. It was rumored that all the river towns, and even New Orleans, were in danger. Leaving the *Josh V. Throop* at the Evansville wharf, Clara went to St. Louis and put out from that port in the steamboat *Mattie Bell,* with a trailing convoy of smaller vessels. The *Mattie Bell* was greatly overloaded, and there was more than a possibility that she might sink or be set afire by the cinders from her belching stacks. Nevertheless, her skipper steered for the lower river, navigating the roaring Mississippi to the delta land, dodging broken levees, nosing in and out of treacherous crevasses, hailed as "the phantom ship of mercy." The Red Cross flag was never reefed; by day and night Clara stood beneath it, slim and erect and indomitable.

Her report, written at Evansville, Indiana, on May 10, 1884, was terse and businesslike: "We had covered the Ohio River from Cincinnati to Cairo and back twice, and the Mississippi from St. Louis to New Orleans, and return—four months on the rivers—and traveled over eight thousand miles, distributed relief in money and estimated material, one hundred and seventy-five thousand dollars—gathered as we used it."

That was the report. Between the lines could be glimpsed the epic of gallantry, of property salvaged, innumerable lives saved, of hope restored to a desolated people.

Clara was seated in a private office of the State Department, across the desk from Mr. Frelinghuysen. Outside the open windows the trees were bright green and the marble of the Monument shimmered stark white in the sunshine.

"You seem tired, Miss Barton. Is it this summer heat of Washington?"

"No," Clara said. "I haven't been well since I came home from the floods. Women are odd and perverse creatures, Mr. Frelinghuysen. An emergency bolsters them, and then, when it's over, they—they dissolve. Or so it is with me, anyway."

"That was a magnificent performance. I think you should have relaxation." The secretary smiled. "I shall play that I'm your physician and prescribe a voyage."

"Indeed? I've just had one."

"Fresh water, yes; and too much of it. But salt water is the thing." He nodded and glanced at some papers before him. "I suppose you know that the International Conference of the Red Cross is to convene in September at Geneva?"

"I was notified."

"Good! Miss Barton, I hereby appoint you as a delegate to the Conference."

"No, Mr. Frelinghuysen. Somebody should go; we must be represented. But not *I*."

"You are the very one," he said emphatically. "Who else sufficiently understands our American organization? This is the first convention in which our government shall participate; and we cannot afford to make a mistake in the selection of our delegates. I have thought of naming Judge Joseph Sheldon and Mr. A. S. Solomon also. They will accompany you, but you will be our chief representative and lead the delegation."

"I'd be so—so frightened," she murmured.

"*Frightened?*" The secretary laughed. "You? Why, you're never frightened!"

"I always am."

"Just the same, this is a patriotic duty which you cannot

evade. Therefore, I do appoint you. Please say that you will go, Miss Barton."

She was briefly silent. Then, "I'll go," she said.

The Atlantic was smooth as glass. She was not ill an hour. Mr. Frelinghuysen had told her she would be expected to speak at the Conference, and so she spent most of several days writing, preparing her manuscript. On the last night out, she attended the reception in the ship's palatial salon and consented to read the manuscript to her fellow passengers who had been eagerly wishing to see and hear her.

Landing at Liverpool, the American delegates proceeded directly to Geneva. And there Clara was joined by Antoinette Margot.

"Dear Miss Barton!" Antoinette exclaimed. "I will be your interpreter, your maid—anything. You will surely need me for *something*."

Clara kissed her cheek affectionately. "Thank you, Antoinette. You will be of the greatest help to me."

It was the evening of the Conference's opening session. Clara was on her way to the convention hall. Earlier she had been welcomed to Geneva by elaborate ceremonies which made her rather nervous, but now that the moment for her entrance had come, she felt calm and strong.

At the door of the hall she paused.

This would be the most significant happening of her life, for not only would America take its place tonight among the humanitarian nations of the world, but also there would be adopted here what was known as the American amendment to the Red Cross constitution, that clause which Clara Barton had originated and framed, providing for the peacetime rendering of relief, a principle which she had manifested in action.

She looked into the enormous room. It was brilliantly illuminated, resplendent with color, from the crimson velvet hangings at the windows to the flower-twined crystal candelabra. Strolling about or standing in groups were the delegates of other republics, kingdoms and empires; men of wisdom, power, prestige; the highest-ranking officials of armies, navies, and civil professions. Some of them were in glittering uniforms; many wore jeweled decorations or ribbons crisscrossing their shoulders, adorning their snowy shirtfronts. Their mingled voices made a soberly musical rumble as they talked and waited.

What were they waiting for?

A liveried footman bowed before her. "Your name, madame?"

She gave it, and the footman turned and cried out:

"Miss Clara Barton."

Instantly the throng swung toward her; the hall was hushed. She stepped over the threshold—and, shattering the spell, a full-throated, tremendous shout went up, shaking the very rafters:

"Mademoiselle Barton bien mérité de l'humanité!"

It was a tribute, a phrase of honor like no other in the French language—and probably no woman ever was so hailed before.

"But they're not honoring me," she said to herself. "Not me, but my country."

Little and modest and unassuming, black-haired and simply dressed, smiling a bit, she stood quietly, one woman among four hundred men, and thought about her country, the America she had loved and served, which was here asserting its rightful equality in the fraternity of civilized nations. For how long and with what ardor she had dreamed of this!

"*Vive l'Etats-Unis!*" they were crying. "*Vive!*"

She knew then that her dream was reality.

EPILOGUE

THAT was not the end, of course, but only another of Clara's beginnings.

With her to guide it, the American Red Cross was destined for a heroic future. During the next decade its annals included such events as the Texas famine of 1885; the Charleston earthquake of 1886; the tornado at Mt. Vernon, Illinois, in 1888; the Florida yellow-fever epidemic of that same year; the Johnstown flood in 1889; the tornado at Pomeroy, Iowa, in 1893; the hurricane and tidal wave in the South Carolina islands in 1893 and 1894; the Galveston storm in 1900; the typhoid-fever epidemic at Butler, Pennsylvania, in 1904. At most of these woeful scenes, Clara Barton was present, personally administrating. Each situation she met with her inimitable shrewdness, honesty, compassion, and tact.

Nor did the American Red Cross limit its generosity to domestic crises. In 1896, when the Armenian massacres had terrified a part of Turkey, Clara, as an emissary of good will, went to Asia Minor. There she consulted with Tewfick Pasha, the Turkish Minister of State in Constantinople, convinced him that her plan for the rehabilitation of the agricultural regions was sound and practicable, earned his trust and friendship—and, as testimony of that bond, received medals from the Sultan and from His Royal Highness, the Prince of Jerusalem, Cyprus, and Armenia.

In 1898, when Spain was subduing the insurrection in Cuba, President McKinley authorized the sending of a Red Cross expedition to the besieged and famishing Cubans. The ship sailed for Havana; Clara disembarked there, and shortly after witnessed the tragic sinking of the *U.S.S. Maine,* which was the spark touching off the Spanish-American War. Clara left Havana with the outbreak of hostilities, but soon she was back where the smoke of cannon was thickest, caring for the wounded at Siboney, El Caney, San Juan. For miles, sitting upright in an army lorry, she jolted through sand and stubble —and thought, perhaps, of Virginia's rocky roads, of Falmouth and the Fredericksburg heights. For hours, under the sun, in the rain, she nursed and bandaged, helped men to live or to die, cooked pots of gruel over a stubborn fire—and remembered Antietam, remembered Chantilly and Morris Island.

At Siboney, her hospital was beside the tent of Major Leonard Wood, whom she knew and liked so well. And one day a comrade of Major Wood's, a soldier in rough khaki, a red bandanna draped from his hat, a sack in his hand, pushed in to confront her.

"I've some sick men in my regiment. They want such delicacies as you have here. I'll pay for them out of my own pocket. I suppose I can buy them?"

"Not for a million dollars."

"I *need* these things." His pugnacious face darkened. "I think a great deal of my men, I'm proud of them."

"And so are we proud, sir," Clara said. "But we cannot sell hospital delicacies. We give them."

Chuckling, stuffing his canvas sack, Colonel Theodore Roosevelt stamped off, into the moist, tropic jungle.

Clara was at Santiago, her vessel, the *State of Texas,* the first to steam into the harbor after the mines had been lifted, preceding even the admiral's flagship.

That was a hot, sultry day, the sea flat and iridescent. The war was over, and Clara mused, "War! Through and through —thought and act—body and soul—I hate it!" She turned abruptly from the rail where she had been standing, her eyes on the horizon. "Is there anyone here who can lead us in singing the Doxology?"

"Praise God, from whom all blessings flow . . ."

Reverently they sang it, and then another and as dear an anthem:

> "My country, 'tis of thee,
> Sweet land of liberty . . ."

She was seventy-seven then, spare and straight and agile, with the habit of sitting on the floor, cross-legged, in moments of concentration. Old, was she? No one considered her as that; she seemed not to age or change. It was, her friends said, almost as if she had found that treasure beyond price, the fountain of eternal youth.

A reporter, interviewing her at that time, described her as "a woman of fifty or thereabouts. Her hair is that rare thing in nature—raven black."

"Humph!" said Clara when she read the article. "I have one gray hair—but I've forgotten just where it is."

In her eighty-fifth year, she was pictured by another journalist as "middle-aged." She was in Worcester that summer and protesting to some solicitous relative, "How can you insult one so young as I by asking her to rest in the middle of the afternoon?" And then, more sharply, "Are you in your right mind to ask *me* to rest?"

She would never admit to even a vestige of unusual ability. "I know nothing remarkable I have done. The humdrum

work of my everyday life seems to me quite without incident."
And she was heard to complain, "One of the griefs of my life
is to see other persons getting things done—really done—and
I accomplish so little. I don't see how they do it!"

In 1897 Clara had taken up residence in Glen Echo, Maryland, seven miles from Washington in a house which was the
National Headquarters of the American Red Cross and, henceforth, her home: a queer, boat-shaped structure, designed by
Clara to fit her own notions of usefulness rather than classic
beauty. Here, by day and by night, she worked like a Trojan,
and from its portals sallied out on her errands on this continent and abroad.

In 1887 she had represented the United States at the convention of the International Red Cross in Karlsruhe, and visited
(to her inexpressible delight) with the Grand Duke and the
Grand Duchess of Baden, and chatted genially with the
Emperor and Empress of Germany, with Prince von Bismarck
and Count von Moltke. Ten years later she was attending the
Vienna convention; in 1902 she went to St. Petersburg, Russia,
on a similar mission. The governments of a score of nations
bestowed upon her medals and decorations, which she cherished but seldom wore.

In 1904 she resigned from the presidency of the American
Red Cross. She did this voluntarily, though with sincere regret.
Previous to her decision to resign, there had been some criticism, not general yet unpleasant, of her management of the
organization's affairs. It was said of Clara that she was too
dictatorial and had too much power. At the start she had
centered all control in her hands, and she obdurately kept it so.
A few contributors of funds thought that the work of the
society in the Spanish-American War had fallen short of the

standards, and Clara herself was dissatisfied with the showing made in the Galveston flood disaster. Since that time grumblings had recurred, some of them spiteful and most of them unjustified, as to Clara's direction.

The fact was that by 1904 the Red Cross had grown to colossal size, outstripping even Clara Barton's dream of it. The methods of administration of the old days, when it was young and small, no longer sufficed. Now it must be reincorporated on a more extensive and detailed plan.

Clara was slow to see this; at last she was convinced. A salaried post as honorary president was offered her, but she refused. Somewhat sadly, as at Bordentown in the far-off past, she "relinquished the helm."

The reincorporation occurred by Act of Congress in January 1905, and William Howard Taft, then Secretary of War, was elected president of the Red Cross, an office he continued to occupy during his Presidency of the United States. With Taft was established the tradition which Clara Barton had proposed when she had wished that Garfield, as President of the United States, be also president of her infant organization. Like so many other of her precepts and policies, this one has persisted.

She had viewed at close range and had been in contact with every President since 1861—Lincoln, Johnson, Grant, Hayes, Garfield, Arthur, Cleveland, Harrison, McKinley, Theodore Roosevelt. She had known them all, and some she had admired more than others—she had had her favorites among them. Yet she had an instinctive veneration for the exalted place held by these men. It was well, she thought, that such leaders should command the cause she had begun and fostered.

Her path had not always been strewn with roses. Occasionally she had been weary. But having retired, she discovered that leisure bored her. She carried on a huge correspondence, for she adored letter writing, but this was not enough to occupy her. She founded the National First Aid Association of America, which, legally incorporated, had its headquarters in Boston. She served as national chaplain of the Woman's Relief Corps. Each year she was the guest of honor at encampments of the Grand Army of the Republic.

In 1910, when she was eighty-nine, Clara traveled alone to Chicago, enjoying the trip and the round of breakfasts, teas, and receptions given for her. Each day she shook hands with thousands of people. With a fine, resonant voice she spoke in churches and auditoriums where people crowded to hear her.

On her way home in the autumn, she stopped in Boston to inquire what had happened at the First Aid during her absence. A clergyman friend of the Barton family was startled that day to see Clara on the curb of the traffic-packed street; he darted forward to escort her. But a helmeted police sergeant was before him, and Clara tucked her little gloved hand into the policeman's arm. She waved to her friend—and waved him aside. He followed and caught up with her on the opposite curb.

"My dear Miss Clara, what are you doing here?"

"I'm just taking the streetcar to Worcester. It's a distance of only forty miles."

"Officer," said the clergyman, "I thank you and all the country thanks you for your courtesy to this lady. Do you know who she is? Miss Clara Barton."

"Indade an' indade!" exclaimed the burly sergeant. "The greatest little lady in America!"

In January 1911 she was invited by the *Review of Reviews* to write an article on "Hospitals and Hospital Nurses of the Civil War." She declined, saying she knew nothing about the subject. In April she finished her *History of the Red Cross.* That month also she commenced the study of tree grafting. It was a thing she often had wanted to learn. She was reading diligently, all sorts of literature. And she was much interested in the candidacy of William Jennings Bryan for the Presidency. "If we must have a Democrat," she said, "he will do very well." In May she wrote her will, commented on the suffrage parade in London, and said that woman suffrage, in which she had long believed, would be a blessing—but not an unmixed blessing. She did not fancy the styles, either: the women's huge hats and really dangerous hatpins, the hobble and harem skirts. She salted down eggs in the early summer, and during July and August she did most of her own cooking.

In the autumn she was rather sick, yet in mid-December she issued a message of Christmas peace to all the world. "I am feeling much better today," she said, "and have every hope of spending a pleasant and joyful Christmas when I shall celebrate my ninetieth birthday." And it *was* a happy birthday.

But with the new year she was ill again and could not rally. At last, in March, her marvelous vitality seemed to ebb. She saw Palm Sunday pass and then Easter Sunday.

On the night of April 10, she roused from sleep. "I thought I was on the battlefield," she said. "The poor boys were lying on the cold ground, with no nurses and no physicians to do anything for them. I saw the surgeons coming, and too much needed by all to give special attention to any one. . . . Then I woke to hear myself groan because I have a stupid pain in my back. Here on a good bed with every attention! I am ashamed that I murmur!"

On April 12, 1912, in the morning, she whispered those words she had so often uttered, and this time finally:

"Let me go! *Let me go!*"

But even this was not the end, for she had belonged and still belongs to that select company of American immortals whose glory cannot fade or perish. While the country she loved exists, while the scarlet and white banner of the Red Cross floats beside the Stars and Stripes, then and always will Clara Barton live.

BIBLIOGRAPHY

Adams, James Truslow: *History of the United States.* New York: Charles Scribner's Sons, 1933.

Bacon-Foster, Corra: *Clara Barton, Humanitarian* (Collection, Library of Congress). Columbia Historical Society, 1918.

⭐ Barton, Clara: *The Red Cross in Peace and War.* American Historical Press, 1899.

———*A Story of the Red Cross.* New York: D. Appleton and Company, 1918.

———*The Story of My Childhood.* New York: The Baker and Taylor Company, 1907.

Barton, William E.: *The Life of Clara Barton* (2 vols.). Boston: Houghton Mifflin Company, 1922.

Boardman, Mabel T.: *Under the Red Cross Flag.* Philadelphia: J. B. Lippincott Company, 1915.

Brockett, L. P., and Vaughan, Mary C.: *Woman's Work in the Civil War* (With an Introduction by Henry W. Bellows, D.D.). Philadelphia: Bradley and Company, 1867.

Butler, Benjamin F.: *Butler's Book.* Boston: A. M. Thayer and Company, 1892.

Dennett, Tyler, selected by: *Lincoln and the Civil War,* In the Diaries and Letters of John Hay. New York: Dodd, Mead and Company, 1939.

Dock, Lavinia L., Pickett, Sara Elizabeth, Noyes, Clara D., Clement, Fannie F., Fox, Elizabeth G., and Van Meter, Anna R.: *History of American Red Cross Nursing.* New York: The Macmillan Company, 1922.

Encyclopædia Britannica.

Epler, Percy H.: *The Life of Clara Barton.* New York: The Macmillan Company, 1917.

Great Debates in American History, Vol. 6. New York: Current Literature Publishing Company, 1913.

Haley, William D., ed.: *Philp's Washington Described.* New York: Rudd and Carleton, 1861.

Harper's Weekly. Vols. XXIV, XXV, XXVI, and the Special Edition for Friday, July 8, 1881.

Hart, Albert Bushnell, ed.: *The American Nation, A History.* New York: Harper and Brothers, 1907.

Moss, Reverend Lemuel: *Annals of the U. S. Christian Commission.* Philadelphia: J. B. Lippincott Company, 1868.

Shaw, Albert: *Abraham Lincoln, The Year of His Election.* New York: Review of Reviews Corporation, 1930.

ALSO

Adams, Elmer C., and Foster, Warren Dunham: *Heroines of Modern Progress.* New York: Sturgis and Walton Company, 1913. Pages 147-177.

America's Twelve Great Women Leaders. Associated Authors Service, 1933.

Gordy, Wilbur F.: *Our Patriots.* New York: Charles Scribner's Sons, 1918. Pages 154-162.

Hagedorn, Hermann: *The Book of Courage.* Philadelphia: John C. Winston Company, 1930. Pages 199-212.

Herzberg, Max: *Americans in Action.* New York: D. Appleton Century Company, 1937. Pages 290-296.

Howe, M. E. DeWolfe: *Causes and Their Champions.* Boston: Little, Brown and Company, 1926. Pages 3-43.

Humphrey, Grace: *Women in American History.* Indianapolis: Bobbs-Merrill Company, 1919. Pages 189-206.

Larcom, Lucy: "Clara Barton," in *Our Famous Women.* Hartford: A. D. Worthington and Company, 1884. Pages 94-116.

McCallum, Jane Y.: *Women Pioneers.* Johnson Publishing Company, 1929. Pages 127-138.

Moore, Rebecca: *When They Were Girls.* Owen Publishing Company, 1923. Pages 37-44.

Morris, Charles: *Heroes of Progress in America.* Philadelphia: J. B. Lippincott Company, 1906. Pages 317-324.

Murphy, Mable Ansley: *Greathearted Women*. Philadelphia: The Union Press, 1920. Pages 59-64.

Parkman, Mary R.: *Heroines of Service*. New York: The Century Company, 1917. Pages 61-85.

Tappan, Eva March: *Heroes of Progress*. Boston: Houghton Mifflin Company, 1921. Pages 140-146.

Vocations, Vol. VI. Boston: Hall and Locke, 1911. Pages 248-261.

Wade, Mary H.: *The Light-Bringers*. Boston: Little, Brown and Company, 1914. Pages 64-111.

About the Author

JEANNETTE COVERT NOLAN was born in Indiana and has lived there all her life. Her forebears came there as pioneers, and her grandfather owned one of the first newspapers in the state. Her father and brother were newspaper men, and this influenced her to become a writer. On graduation from high school, she worked as a reporter for the Evansville *Courier* until she married. After her children were grown, she turned seriously to writing books, the first of which was published in 1932. Since then she has been very active writing short stories, plays, essays, fiction and biography. She taught creative writing at Indiana University and conducted juvenile workshops at the University of Colorado Writers' Conference. Many of her books have been selected by the Junior Literary Guild, and she was recently voted the outstanding "Hoosier Children's Book Author of the Year."